TIME MANAGEMENT - THE SID™ WAY

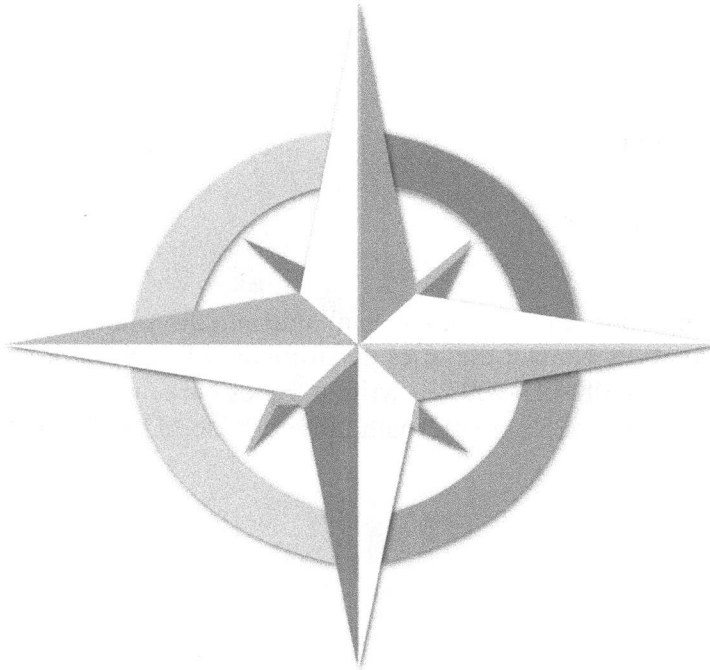

A Self-Initiated Development Workbook for Leaders and Managers

Ben McDonald

Sidney McDonald

BENCHMARK
Learning International

TIME MANAGEMENT – THE SID™ WAY
A Self-Initiated Development Workbook for Leaders and Managers

Benchmark Learning International, Boise 83716

http://www.thesidway.com

ISBN-13:9780615485553

ISBN-10:0615485553

Large quantity purchase of this book is available at a discount from the publisher. For more information, contact the sales department at BenchMark Learning International, Inc. 1-208-433-9093 or write to Sales Director, BenchMark Learning International, 5239 Quarterpath Drive, Boise, ID 83716 U.S.A.

Dedicated to Coreena Fauver

She is an inspiration in time management while succeeding with her family, career, and continued professional development.

Table of Contents

Preface

As coaches and leadership consultants, we have found common themes over the years working with leaders and aspiring leaders in their quest for performance improvement. These leaders have contacted us because they want greater effectiveness in their current position or within their organization. As we work with these leaders, we frequently find that what may appear on the surface as a performance need goes deeper as we uncover what is below the surface of the obvious need. This discovery is what really determines the best path toward improving performance effectiveness.

In many cases, a specific performance need is linked with multiple skill sets the leader needs to demonstrate for overall competence and effectiveness in their position. The best way to identify the most strategic and time-efficient method to a performance improvement plan is to fully understand the range of performance gaps related to the specific leader or group of leaders.

Here is an example of how this discovery process helps determine the most efficient way to performance improvement:

A senior leader contacts us because his department is not meeting their revenue objectives and wants us to conduct a workshop on business development. Certainly, we can deliver the business development workshop and hope for the best improvement based on solid business development principles, or we can take a more holistic approach and evaluate the overall competency of the staff involved in meeting these revenue objectives.

The primary goal is to find out not just what knowledge, skills, and behaviors the staff need to meet their revenue objectives, but to also identify the corresponding skills and behaviors that may be impeding their overall performance. Typically, we uncover other areas that are affecting the revenue results, not just a lack of business development knowledge. For example, poor time management and interpersonal skills, inadequate customer focus and planning skills and other competencies related to business development effectiveness.

This overall assessment provides the insight and next steps to the most effective way to improve revenue results for this leader's department. Results with this approach are typically much greater and long-lasting than the training event alone could deliver.

As part of The SID Way Leadership Development Series™, <u>Time Management – The SID Way: A Self-Initiated Development Workbook for Leaders and Managers,</u> we take you through a similar process so that as you embark on your journey in self-initiated development you have the tools and resources to evaluate your leadership skills and behaviors and formulate a tactical development plan to improve your time management effectiveness.

In this workbook we provide you with:
- Self-initiated development techniques using the SID™ Model to help you efficiently manage your leadership development, customized to your needs and goals.
- Techniques to improve your time management and work-life balance skills and behaviors
- Customized development recommendations in time management and work-life balance based on your self assessment results
- Multiple tools and resources to help you grow your time management and work-life balance effectiveness

Current times call for even more focused use of proven measures to stay successful. Now more than ever you must work hard to develop the skills and behaviors to get ahead and thrive as a leader. It has

> **Leaders must manage their time well and achieve a work-life balance that reduces stress and leads to greater productivity.**

always been *your* responsibility; now more than ever it is up to *you*. Using the techniques and development recommendations provided in this workbook, you can become more effective in your management of time and achieve a work-life balance that reduces your stress, increases your productivity, and enables you to have a life outside of work.

The best way to thrive as a leader and have sustainable professional and business results is to self-initiate your own personal leadership development in a thoughtful and systematic approach, and this includes learning time management techniques. This approach is not only valuable for you to improve your effectiveness and to see an increase in your results, but also benefits your organization. If your organization is successful, your position is more secure.

As professional coaches we have seen leaders that have engaged, worked hard, changed needed behaviors and adopted new skills. The results were noticed by others and consequently they were able to advance into new and more rewarding positions. On the other hand, we have also seen leaders who have been complacent in their professional development. Eventually they lose credibility in their position and their results suffer. We have seen leaders who do not strive to manage their time and become overwhelmed with all they need to do. Their work-life balance becomes skewed and their personal life suffers as well.

We have always believed that development and improvement are the responsibility of the individual, even when leadership development opportunities are available, and that an individual can go as far as they want in their career if they have the motivation, tools and skills. Even if you have the most expensive and renowned leadership coach or training program at your disposal, it will do you no good if you do not personally engage. This workbook and the others in our series are the result of that belief and provide you with:

- Vital leadership principles that will fine tune your leadership skills and behaviors
- Processes to follow to achieve success
- Methods to identify your most pressing leadership needs
- Tools and resources to increase your effectiveness

Following our process may not always be easy. It requires honest self assessment, time and disciplined work on your part; however, the rewards will be worth it. We ask that you take a candid look at your time management skills and your work-life balance; and then take action based on what you see. We cannot guarantee success. However, we can guarantee that if you complete this workbook you will know more about yourself and what you need to do to improve your time management skills and become more effective as a leader. We will be your guide and provide the step-by-step coaching as you walk through our self-initiated development model. The effort and results are in your hands.

> **Self-Initiated development requires commitment and hard work on your part. But, we are here to help you along the way.**

We Wrote This Workbook For You!

If you are currently in or aspiring to a leadership or management position, if you have the desire to be successful and make a positive impact in your sphere of influence, this book is for you. If you are in a threatened industry or any organization that is undergoing "belt tightening," self-initiated development is especially important because you need to differentiate yourself from competition. If you have lost your position in leadership or management, what better time than now to methodically work to improve your time management skills and behaviors in preparation for a future position. Finally, if you are successful in your current position and see yourself retiring within the next ten years, this book is vital for you. During the last years of your career it is easy to think you do not need to improve your time management skills or your work-life balance. This can lead to your becoming complacent and burnt-out.

Your Coaching Team

As your coaches throughout this workbook, we will impart not only our knowledge of time management skills and behaviors, but also many of the lessons we have learned from our clients. We, like most others at the onset of a career, began near the bottom of an organization and worked hard while actively engaging in a variety of continuous learning activities. Our careers have taken us through the doors of various industries and organizations, and prior to our own leadership development and coaching practice, included operations, sales and human resources experiences. Within each of these positions and experiences our leadership responsibilities increased, eventually taking us into senior leadership positions.

During the leadership development phase of our careers we began working more closely with leaders in identifying those skills and behaviors that promote effectiveness, results and advancement. Along with extensive research over the past 20 years, we have refined the competencies that successful leaders exemplify and the tools used to promote results within these core competencies. This research and experience are the basis for our leadership competency model which is shown in Appendix D in Part 4 of this book and is the basis of our self-initiated development series of 31 workbooks addressing the most important competencies for leadership and management positions.

A Final Thought Before You Begin

Make the time for yourself to achieve your dreams and success, starting with developing your skills in time management. If you are having difficulty finding the time to develop your skills and behaviors, this is the workbook you should complete first. The principles of time management provided here will help you eliminate that excuse.

YOU are the one responsible for your professional development. Your future is waiting.

Acknowledgments

This book would not be a reality without the unwavering support of many individuals. First, we wish to thank our many clients from whom we have learned so much. It is in their organizations that we have been able to form, test, and improve the concepts used in this book. We do not have the space to name each client and individual but we will personally thank them.

To the hundreds of leaders and managers that we have coached and advised, we thank you for your openness to our style and our pushing you to be your best. We recognize that it is not easy to be coached, but have seen the positive results and achievements you have made. Time management is a recurring theme in our coaching because, regardless of needs in other competencies, the issue of time always comes up.

Our mentors in the past have contributed through pointing out our own self-initiated development paths we have followed. We owe much to some great advocates of time management and work-life balance including, President John Anderson of Illinois Institute of Technology; Betsy Hughes, Vice President of University Advancement, Illinois Institute of Technology; Nancy Atwood; Bill Doherty; and Linda Simmons. We have learned from your successes and respect you all as leaders. Each of these individuals has become expert at their own time management strategies.

Others have contributed to our efforts by reviewing our draft manuscripts or brainstorming ideas with us. A special thanks to Colby Stream for his valuable review and feedback.

As "students of leadership" we have also been influenced by other successful leaders, some of whom we know and others that we simply observe because they are the best at what they do. These include Pastor Paul Hatfield of The Pursuit church in Boise, Idaho, and Coach Chris Petersen of Boise State University.

"Time is what we want most, but what we use worst."
- William Penn

Coaches' Questions to Ponder

Why do you want to develop your time management skills and behaviors?

Do you believe you can improve your work-life balance?

Do you believe that professional development is your responsibility or the responsibility of your organization?

Introduction

Welcome to *Time Management – The SID Way; A Self-Initiated Development Workbook for Leaders and Managers*. Self-Initiated Development (SID™) is the future of learning and achieving your professional goals. Our purpose in developing our SID™ series for leaders and managers is to provide a tool to identify strengths and weaknesses in your professional skills and behaviors and provide a model for you to take charge of your own development.

The following FAQs will help you better understand SID™ and the role of this time management workbook.

Who Should Use Self-Initiated Development?

SID™ is designed for you to take charge of your own professional development and can be used alone or in conjunction with other development tools; so the simple answer to who should use self-initiated development – anyone who wants to improve their professional skills and achieve their goals. This certainly includes those who have a need to improve their time management skills and their work-life balance.

Many people say, "But I have a degree." Or, "My company provides training for me to improve." In response to these questions, anyone with at least a day of experience in a company or organization knows there is much more to learn than what they received from their degree program. What they have learned may be valuable, but there is so much more to learn about application, skills and behaviors that higher education cannot address.

> **Self-Initiated Development is based on your needs. You provide the commitment and initiative, we provide the tools.**

Additionally, most experienced professionals realize that while their company may provide some training, they are not typically capable of handling all leadership development activities, and in today's economic climate fewer and fewer companies and organizations are providing sufficient leadership and management training programs. It is a simple economic fact that when times are lean, professional development is one of the first areas to be cut. We believe that whether professional development is provided by your organization or not, YOU are the one responsible for improving and achieving your goals. SID™ will help you do that and clearly differentiate you from others.

How Does This Workbook Fit Into the Overall SID™ Program?

SID™ is a proven development process; this workbook is a tool to help you achieve better time management and work-life balance as part of that process. We have developed over thirty workbooks to supplement the SID™ process for leaders. You can select which workbooks to use based on your self assessment across each of the 30 leadership competencies. More about the SID™ process will come later. We will also give you extensive guidance on how to use this workbook to achieve the maximum benefit on your route to achieving your time management and work-life balance goals.

How Did We Select the 30 Leadership Competencies?

We have a combined 40 years experience in leadership development, working with corporate, non-profit and university organizations. Our selection of the most relevant competencies comes from our experience in giving online leadership assessments, presenting workshops and facilitating retreats for leadership teams around the world. In addition, we have reviewed most of the "literature" and models that have been published over the past 20 years. We are confident that our broad look at the competencies that make up leadership skills and behaviors is the best approach to take to provide readers with targeted goals to improve their leadership skills.

Our 30 competencies are organized using our 4P's Competency Model™ which is represented by a compass. The competencies are divided between each of the four compass heading titles. Time Management is in the Positive Results compass heading. To see the complete model with the competencies assigned to each "P," refer to Appendix E. We encourage you to review this list and order the workbooks most appropriate to your position and professional goals.

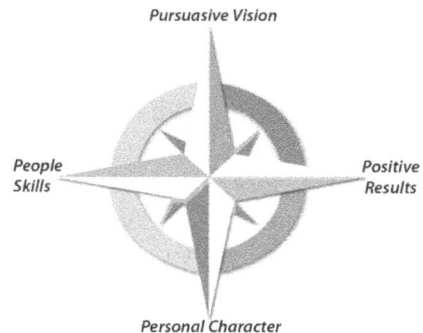

4P's Leadership Competency Model™

You can also contact us at questions@thesidway.com to receive a copy of our master self assessment. By completing this master self assessment, you can determine which competencies are your strengths and which are the areas you should most focus on improving.

How is this Workbook Organized?

There are four distinct parts to the workbook. First, you will be given an overview of our Self-Initiated Development (SID™) model and be introduced to how it can help you identify, assess and improve in the competencies needed for your current and/or future position.

The second part of the workbook provides the content, exercises and case studies that are at the heart of your efforts to improve your time management behaviors. You should spend most of your time with this section of the workbook.

The third part to the workbook provides the specific recommendations and tools you need to complete a development plan to achieve your goals.

The final part is the appendices, which include tools you can use in the future and the "Coaches' Bookshelf," providing additional reading resources to help you further advance your time management skills and behaviors.

In summary, the workbook is organized as follows:

- Part 1 – The SID™ Model
- Part 2 – Time Management
- Part 3 – Development Recommendations
- Part 4 - Appendices, including Takeaway Tools and the Coaches' Bookshelf

What is Our Coaching Approach to Developing Leaders in this Workbook?

The content in this book is designed for you to learn more about time management and work-life balance yourself. However, our role is to be your "Coach." We are leadership coaches and have found in our work that self-initiated development may not be the only choice you have to improve your skills, but it may be the best method for you to learn.

As your coaches, we recommend that you read the content and do all the exercises in the order provided. The "How to Use the Time Management Workbook" section provides valuable suggestions on how to use this book, particularly Parts 2 and 3. If you have any questions, feel free to e-mail your question to questions@thesidway.com. One of your coaches will get back to you within 24 hours with a response.

"I am still learning."
- Michelangelo

Coaches' Questions to Ponder

How do you think better time management skills and behaviors will improve your work-life balance?

Who has helped you in your personal development? Who has helped you in your professional development? How did they do this? Were you receptive?

What attempts have you made in the past to develop your leadership skills and behaviors? Have they been successful? What could you have done differently?

Do you see a correlation between self-initiated development and success in those you have observed during your career?

Part 1 – The Self-Initiated Development (SID™) Model

*"Life is a classroom. Only those who are willing to
be lifelong learners will move to the head of the class."*
- Zig Ziglar

As you will learn in a moment, professional development is an ongoing process and its initiation and completion is up to YOU. You can become a better leader if YOU desire; you will have difficulty if you lack the initiative or the desire.

Our SID™ model stresses the importance of taking responsibility for your own development and provides a framework for your development efforts. Following this straight-forward development process, that you are in charge of and accountable to, gives you a path to increase your effectiveness as a leader or manager.

Self-Initiated Development Background

Self-initiated development is a principle that is at the very fabric of our world from its inception and is a critical component for personal and professional success. For centuries, people have had to be self-reliant in many areas of life to succeed, and in some cases to even survive. There are countless examples of people in history and in the present day that have had a vision, determined a path to achieve their vision, and have done the work necessary to succeed; sometimes at much effort, trial and error, and sacrifice. Although working with others toward achieving common goals is also a critical factor to achieving success, without individual motivation and drive along a pre-determined path, our outcomes can be severely thwarted and stalled.

From the beginning, others help in our development. When we are small children our parents help us with everything, even eating and learning how to go to the toilet. As we become older we still get help developing from teachers, family and coaches. Others help us develop in a myriad of ways – physically, emotionally and intellectually; and for some, spiritually. Even in college we develop with the help of our professors and teaching assistants. Then we get to our first "real" job. Many organizations have programs for entry-level employees, but often we develop through on-the-job training. Then, as we gain experience and combine it with the right attitudes and skills, we are promoted to more challenging positions and we continue to refine our skills and influence through further development.

Self-initiated and directed development is a powerful force. As Carl Rogers, an eminent psychologist asserted, "Anything that can be taught to another is relatively inconsequential, and has little or no significant influence on behavior." Likewise, he adds, "The only learning which significantly influences behavior is self-discovered self-appropriated learning."

A valid example of the power self-initiated development can be seen in Abraham Lincoln's life. He confirms the concept of self-initiated development and success when he said to "bear in mind, your own resolution to succeed is more important than any other one thing." He goes further to say of himself that, "I'll study and prepare, and when the time comes I'll be ready." This philosophy and drive were part of the reason for his great success despite a marginal formal education.

Development is a life-long process and involves many facets of learning. For success to be achieved during this process we have to be self-disciplined, motivated and, if possible, identify our ultimate goal. For that reason, we have created a self-initiated development process that through years of research and working with leaders has proven to help people achieve their success and advance in their profession.

Self-Initiated vs. Organizational-Initiated Development

In many ways, our changing culture has given us messages that are not always conducive to self-initiated development. We have become reliant on others to tell us what we should do and set the path for us. In essence our reliance has shifted from ourselves to others, often unintentionally, in the organization we are associated. As previously mentioned, it is important to have others involved in achieving great outcomes; however, the subtle message we often get is that "we" will do it for you, just follow "our" plan.

One example of this can be found in the organizational setting by well meaning organizations bringing employee and leadership development to new levels in order to raise the talent of their workforce. Rightfully so, this has been and still is a necessary component in an ever-changing and competitive landscape. However, the dilemma is that over the years employees have often become reliant on their employer for professional development and the path toward professional success. Consequently, in many cases individual motivation for growth dwindles as it becomes a "have to" training and development event rather than a personal "passion" to grow and achieve greater things for self and organization.

In addition, today's economy is driving many organizations to eliminate costly training and development programs. However, this does not eliminate an individual's need to continually improve their skills and behaviors to become a better leader. That is why sustainable development must now focus on "self initiation."

Self-initiated development is not meant to replace organizational development initiatives and is not meant to promote a "lone ranger" mentality that abandons the importance of teamwork endeavors; after all, in business and in life we need others and those we work with are important in our career success and many times to our professional advancement. When looking at an organization's development initiatives it is wise for us to remember that the organization cannot provide all things for our development. Organizational development programs are often at the mercy of the organization's leaders, its ability to fund these initiatives, and are confined to the culture within which they are constructed. Therefore, this gives us even more reason to take our professional development and success into our own hands because, ultimately, we are in control and can shape the outcome and keep it sustainable.

Who Should Initiate Self Development?

So how do we weave the concept of self-initiated development into our current situation so that we may advance from where we are now and set ourselves on a path that leads us to reach our professional goals? The first important key to remember is that it is about *your* development, *your* passions, *your* goals and *your* success. The bottom line is that you are a unique individual with goals, dreams and aspirations as well as talents, strengths and certainly a few weaknesses. You know where you want to go in your professional life (together with or separate from your current employer), what interests you, and may even have an idea of the path toward goal achievement. The model to follow for self-initiated development is meant to support you in achieving your goals through a systematic process in which you are in control; therefore, you control the outcome (and success) as well. You have full responsibility for the process and can take it as far as you need or desire.

So who should initiate and direct their own professional development? The answer is everyone! Young, old, successful, self-employed, unemployed, students, leaders of organizations and anyone else aspiring to be successful or advance their career should be on a systematic process for self-development. It is important to remember that no one is going to do it for you, although you may have guides along the way to provide assistance. If your job title or function is like any of the following, this book is for you:

- Executives and other senior leaders (C-level, V.P. level, Director level)
- General manager
- Project manager
- Sales manager
- Technical manager
- Training manager
- Team leader
- Entrepreneur and small business owner
- Business development manager
- Anyone aspiring to the above positions

Different organizations (corporations, higher education, government, non-profit, entrepreneur) may have different titles, but you get the picture. Anyone who is in a leadership or management position (or those who aspire to these positions) will benefit from this book.

One of the goals of this book is to challenge your paradigms around how to achieve professional growth and advancement as well as provide a framework and the supporting tools in which you can be personally responsible for realizing your professional success. Most important, we hope to encourage the growth of our current and future leaders; for with you at your best, our businesses, schools and non-profit organizations will be more successful and your impact can and will make a positive difference in our world.

Self-Initiated Development vs. Self Improvement

Some may point out that there are hundreds, if not thousands, of books and articles on how to improve. Primarily, these resources focus on your self improvement. Although we advocate self improvement to develop yourself as a well-balanced person, our focus is on the specific skills and behaviors needed in your professional life. Few books or articles exist that clearly give the professional effective steps to own their professional development and succeed at achieving professional goals.

Examples may be in order to clarify the differences between self-initiated development and self improvement, specifically when it comes to time management and work-life balance.

First, an example of self-initiated development:

Lily was new in her position as a project manager. She had been to workshops on project management and had gained her certification as a Project Management Professional. She had no idea, however, that a real project management position would be so consuming. There were actually days when she was in meetings all day, with no time to do her normal work. Her only solution was to take hours of work home each night and weekends. This was the only way it seemed she could keep her head above water.

She observed a few of her colleagues and one stood out to her. Josh never seemed to take work home and he always managed to have everything done. She rationalized this by thinking that Josh gained time by skipping many of the meetings she was attending. Finally, she talked with Josh and asked him how he did it.

"Effective time management," was his brief answer. Lily knew she had a problem with time, but didn't realized she had a problem with time management. Josh pointed her to a time management self assessment and encouraged her to take it. When she did, she was amazed at what it told her. She knew she needed to take steps to improve immediately, or face the fact that she would always be working hours each evening at home and all day Saturday.

Lily created a development plan to target two behaviors to change each week. Over the next month her efficiency improved and some days she was able to leave without any evening work to do. By the end of the third month, people were asking her how she managed to get all her work done and not be burdened with work each evening.

Self improvement is somewhat different, as this example illustrates:

Dale repeatedly missed deadlines and it infuriated his boss, Natasha. When he missed the deadline for the SinCo proposal and the company lost an opportunity to win a $5M contract, Natasha saw it as the last straw. She told Dale he was on probation and if any deadlines were missed in the future he would be out the door. Dale's only response was that he has too much to do and he worked hard every night and almost every weekend.

Meanwhile, on the home front, Dale was getting a lot of heat. His wife was complaining that he worked every night and missed all his daughters' school events. Every time he promised to keep a weekend free to devote to his family he reneged on it at the last moment.

Dale knew he needed to do something...and quick! He reviewed his task list and began to delegate more tasks to his team. He learned of a time management workshop at a local hotel and signed up to go. While the program was going on he was sitting in the back multi-tasking – something he was proud of, feeling he was accomplishing two things at once. He did pick up some time management tips that he adopted; but not nearly as many as he would have if he had been paying attention.

Things began to get better and he didn't miss a deadline for a few weeks. He managed to go to a few school events and even took a weekend off to take the family to the city for shopping and a play.

Although Dale was proud of himself, he was also frustrated. He was meeting deadlines, but only because he was able to delegate much of his work. He didn't take work home much anymore, so he felt imprisoned at home – there was nothing to do except talk with his kids and his wife – and that got boring real quick.

Soon, Dale began to slip back into his old habits. He would take work home and tell his wife that it was critical for him to do it – after all, she didn't want him to lose his job, did she? He began delegating less, telling himself that only he could do certain projects.

By the end of the third month he missed two important deadlines and Natasha fired him.

What are the differences between these two situations? First, Lily recognized that although she had the needed skills for project management, she would fail in her job if she did not improve her time management behaviors. In Dale's case, his improvement was necessitated because of poor performance and problems in his personal life. Lily developed objectives and took steps to get an objective assessment of her strengths and weaknesses in time management. Dale simply went to a workshop to get hints on doing better in one particular area. Lily achieved her goal through using a myriad of developmental resources to progress methodically along her long-term path. Dale became complacent again after he got through his immediate crisis. He returned to the place of most comfort.

Self-initiated development is an active process leading toward a professional goal. It is positive. Self improvement, although the outcome may be positive in some ways, focuses on correcting (often due to the demands of others) a negative attribute.

The SID™ Model

As coaches, we have developed a holistic approach to leadership development using the SID™ model (shown on page 18) to enable individuals to increase their effectiveness. The model, although simple and straightforward, does require one key ingredient on behalf of the participant – motivation. The

Part 1 – The Self-Initiated Development (SID) Model

SID™ model provides the guidelines and framework; you provide the motivation and self discipline to succeed. On the following pages, after the model, we explain more about each step.

Self-Initiated Development Model (SID™)

Where do you want to be in one year? Five years? Ten years?

Determine Your Goals

What skills are needed to attain your goals? What skills do you need now?

Identify Present and Future Competencies

What are your current strengths and weaknesses as viewed by others?

Assess Your Current State

What do you need to achieve to reach your goals?

Develop Objectives to Achieve Goals

Step-by-step directions to achieve your objectives and goals.

Create a Development Action Plan

Put your plan into action and stay motivated!

Implement Development Action Plan

Time and Commitment

SUCCESS!

Step One – Determine Your Goals

Have you given thought to your future goals? Can you clearly articulate them? Have you given much thought to where you want to be in a year? Five years? Ten years? Many people have a muddled sense of where they want to be, but are not clear about either their goals or the path to get there.

We recommend that you give a lot of thought during the initial phase of self-initiated development to your personal and professional goals for the future. Goals should be realistic, both conceptually and from a time perspective. It is not realistic to set a goal to become the CEO of a Fortune 500 company in the next year if you are currently a mid-level manager in a small company. Be realistic when setting your goals.

Explore what makes you happy and fills your day with joy and energy. Perhaps your goals should be more aligned with your happiness than the financial compensation.

Personal Reflection

Using the following chart, list your future goals for 1 year, 2 years, 5 years, and 10 years.

	GOAL
1 YEAR	
1 YEAR	
1 YEAR	
1 YEAR	
2 YEARS	

2 YEARS	
2 YEARS	
2 YEARS	
5 YEARS	
5 YEARS	
5 YEARS	
10 YEARS	
10 YEARS	
10 YEARS	

After thinking about your goals, write a paragraph about each. Then, list the benefits of achieving each goal. The better you can articulate a goal and its benefits, the easier it's going to be to take the steps to achieve it and maintain your motivation.

Step Two – Identify Present and Future Competencies

A competency is a skill, attitude or behavior that is required to do a particular job. Although a job may require some technical competencies, we are currently concerned with those that are management or leadership oriented. Entry-level competencies may include problem solving, communications, teamwork and integrity. More senior-level positions may include competencies such as strategic thinking, motivation, conflict management and influencing. Competencies are position specific and often identified in a person's job description.

For self-initiated development we encourage participants to not only identify and assess their performance on competencies for their current position but also the position they may aspire to attain. This gives a more thorough perspective in preparing for the future.

Competencies are measured using assessment items. A group of items measure each competency. For example, an item that measures communication skills may be: *Develops excellent customer presentations.* Other communication items would be included in the assessment that would measure other aspects of communication skills, such as written communications, oral communications and client/customer communication skills.

By identifying your present and future competency needs you can have a clear understanding of what is required for you to be effective and successful in your current and desired positions. Remember, these competencies are those skills and behaviors you need to do well to be successful in your current or desired position.

Personal Reflection

Review the following list of competencies. Check which apply to your current position and which apply to a position to which you aspire.

COMPETENCY	APPLIES TO CURRENT POSITION (√)	APPLIES TO DESIRED POSITION (√)
Business Development		
Change Leadership		
Commitment to Diversity		
Commitment to Quality		
Communication		
Conflict Management		
Courage		
Creativity		
Credibility		
Customer Focus		
Decision Making		
Financial Management		
Focus on Results		
Followership		
Influencing		
Initiative		
Inspiration		
Integrity		
Interpersonal Skills		
Motivation		
Negotiation		
Planning		
Problem Solving		
Strategic Thinking		
Stress Management		
Talent Management		
Teamwork		
Technical Skills		
Time Management		
Trust		

These competencies are covered in the BenchMark Learning International workbook series. We recommend that you complete the master self assessment on our website (www.thesidway.com) to determine your strengths and which areas you should focus on improving. The remainder of this book provides the content and exercises to improve your time management skills and behaviors.

Step 3 – Assess Your Current State

The third step of the SID™ model is to assess your current state for each competency either through a self assessment or a 360° assessment that solicits feedback from a larger group of people. The "Know Your Heading" section in Part 2 of this book includes a self assessment for Time Management. The difficulty with a self assessment is that you must be totally honest and transparent with yourself. The results may be quite different from a 360° assessment, which takes into account the perceptions of others. However, the self assessment is an excellent way to start identifying your strengths and weaknesses. Based on the results of your self assessment you can then move to the next step.

Step 4 – Develop Objectives to Achieve Goals

Develop a set of objectives to improve your skills and behaviors in the competencies you need to focus on. Objectives may be designed to enhance a person's strengths or, more often, to overcome identified weaknesses.

Objectives should be SMART – Specific, Measurable, Attainable, Relevant and Timely. Let's look at SMART objectives in more detail.

Specific – Objectives need to be specific. For example, *I will improve my time management*, is not specific. What part of time management is your weakness? A more specific objective would be: *I will read the developmental recommendations regarding how to communicate more effectively with customers by March 30.*

Measurable – Objectives should be measurable so that you know when they are attained or how much progress is being made. Using our previous example, a measurable objective would be: *I will read the four development recommendations regarding how to communicate more effectively with customers by March 30.* This is measurable; you know how much you have accomplished and how much is remaining to do.

Attainable – Although we have already established that self-initiated development is a lot of work and requires discipline, you must be realistic with what you can accomplish. Try not to focus on too much in too limited time. This will only serve to frustrate you. Stress results, not quantity.

Relevant – Sometimes, we may pursue an avenue that is not relevant to what we want to achieve. Following the general development recommendations provided with each competency will keep your objectives relevant. Be careful and stay focused on what is important to achieve.

Timely – Schedule is important! Evaluate everything you need to do as part of your development plan and realistically schedule the actions you need to take to achieve each objective. In our above example, you would schedule the reading of each of the development recommendations and the date you schedule the last to be finished is the date you will achieve that objective.

Step 5 – Create a Development Action Plan

The most important part of preparing to improve is the developmental action plan. Without a specific plan to follow that includes actions to strengthen and improve in your weakest areas, your efforts may not be focused. Even though you have specific objectives to achieve your goals you may not be successful without a plan. Later in this workbook we will help you create a development action plan based on the results of your self-assessment.

Step 6 – Implementing Your Development Action Plan

Now the hard part begins. The self assessment process is over and you have created your development action plan based on your self assessment scores. If you follow the plan, you will achieve each objective and ultimately your goal. The biggest problems that people encounter when implementing their action plan are that they allow obstacles to steal their time away from the direction of the plan. Or, they are easily distracted because they do not see immediate results. Here are some tips to successfully implement your action plan.

- Set a date to start your development steps for each competency. Mark it on your calendar and make it an important day.

- List your goals and put them in a very visible place so that you see them every day.

- Next to each goal, list the benefits of achieving it. Review the benefits daily.

- When you complete an action step (reading an article or book, completing an exercise) mark it off in your plan.

- Don't get discouraged if you get off schedule. Life happens and we are not always able to stay on schedule. Review your schedule and determine how you can make up time.

- Review the results of your self assessment periodically to reinforce to yourself that you are on the right track.

- Celebrate successes. If you are taking steps to improve your decision making, celebrate when you change behaviors in this area, especially when you see the positive results!

- Share your plan with a family member or trusted colleague. Ask them to be an accountability partner. Meet with them regularly to show your results.

- Don't be afraid to tweak your goals or objectives if you change your direction slightly. New opportunities are always entering our lives and you need to be adaptable.

Final Considerations

Another reason for implementing self-initiated development is competition. In today's world, we face fierce competition and it increases everyday. Competition does not just happen at the organizational level, but also at the individual level. Having the ability to positively differentiate yourself in the "crowd" will only increase your likelihood of reaching your goals (or, in today's environment, maintaining your employment).

When we look at today's world with unknown economic times ahead, we should all prepare to differentiate ourselves because those who are viewed as self-starters, motivated and as having the greatest overall skills and behaviors are the ones that will land the jobs, get the promotions, succeed in their current position, succeed in their small businesses and be able to influence others with integrity to attain success.

Finally, those that initiate and direct their own professional development reap the rewards of success. This certainly may be monetary, but you will also find that these people are usually those that are happy, the highest earners and highly respected by others.

Part 2 – Time Management

Introduction

Being able to effectively manage time has a direct impact on productivity, happiness and success. Leaders must be able to manage their time well because there is so much to do. In addition, leaders have a life outside of work and time management has a direct effect on their work-life balance and their general well-being.

In our coaching practice we rarely meet someone who does not have time management issues or work-life balance issues. As part of our coaching, we always bring the subject up and the response we get from coachees is very telling. All feel they can do better in time management and are relieved to have someone they can talk to about it. Most leaders will only admit they have a time management problem when they are in a safe environment, such as with a coach. Everyone around them may see they have a time management problem or work-life balance problem, but no one brings it up. It is almost as if discussion of time management issues is taboo.

Definition

Time management is the act or process of exercising conscious control over the amount of time spent on specific activities, especially to increase efficiency or productivity. (Wikipedia) A time management system is a designed combination of processes, tools, techniques and methods.

Objectives

This workbook is designed to help you improve your time management skills and behaviors. After reading this book and completing the exercises you will be able to:

- Make the best use of your time

- Make the best use of other's time

- Be consistent in meeting deadlines

- Respond to requests in a timely manner

- Alter your schedule as necessary to address pressing concerns

- Use time management tools to increase and streamline productivity

- Always arrive at meetings and events on time

- Manage meeting agendas appropriately

- Eliminate procrastination

- Say "no" when asked to do tasks that are not in your area of responsibility

- Delegate time-consuming tasks when appropriate

- Use goals, plans and measures to guide efforts

- Eliminate the need to "make work" to avoid difficult tasks

- Use a manageable to-do list focusing on what needs to be done

- Engage in physical activity to stimulate thought processes

- Work reasonable hours

- Reward yourself after an achievement

- Be "present in the moment," whether at work or not at work

- Monitor team members to ensure they have balance

- Enjoy both work and non-work activities

How to Use the Time Management Workbook

In the Time Management workbook it is critical that you "do the work" to get the most out of it. This section describes each part of the workbook and how to use it to learn more about developing exceptional time management skills and behaviors.

As you proceed through the workbook, remember the SID™ model and the importance and process of doing your development activities. Your success depends on the effort that you put into your development.

Coaches' Orientation

This section introduces and defines time management and its importance to a leader. Be sure to read this section first. It also contains a "Coach's Comment." These brief diversions provide you with either an example or personal comment from one of your coaches.

Time Management Behaviors

Learning is all about changing behaviors or attitudes. This section includes an exercise to list what you think are effective and ineffective time management skills and behaviors for a leader. We provide our response to this exercise but please do not turn to our response until you have done the best you can do in listing your ideas on effective and ineffective behaviors. After this exercise you will return to reading more text and examples of time management behaviors.

Map Your Growth Exercise

Our Self-Initiated Development (SID™) program is based on thirty competencies, or skills and behaviors grouped into four behavioral categories, found in our 4P's Competency Model™. The compass at the beginning of this section shows those that are most related to time management. The exercise for this section asks you to describe the relationship between time management and each of the related competencies. We then give you our ideas on the relationship.

The Daily Journey

Before continuing your study of time management we present two case study examples, one demonstrating effective time management, and the second showing ineffective time management skills and behaviors. Following each case study you will respond to questions in "Give Us Your Thoughts." We then provide our responses to each question for you to study in the "Our Thoughts" section. This section gives you the opportunity to think further about effective and ineffective time management skills and behaviors.

What Would You Do?

This section provides examples of poor or ineffective time management skills and behaviors. You are asked to describe what should occur to demonstrate excellent time management behaviors in the situation. Even though some of the examples are "non-business," it is easy to relate the behaviors to your situation. Your Coach then provides thoughts on how the situation should have been handled.

Know Your Heading

At this point in the book, it is time to do your personal work to improve your time management skills and behaviors. The Know Your Heading section is a brief self assessment of how you view *your* time management skills and behaviors. It is important to be as objective as possible and give thought to each item. The table has a list of statements that you will objectively respond to according to the following options:

1	Strongly Disagree
2	Disagree
3	Agree
4	Strongly Agree
N/A	Not applicable to my current position

You will refer to the number in the PG column for each item later when we discuss specific development recommendations for improvement.

Coaches' Guidance

After your self assessment it is time to begin thinking of specific behaviors you can change on your road to improvement. This section highlights specific behaviors you can adopt to improve your time management results
.

Coaches' Itinerary

In Part 3 of this workbook you will find the heart of our Self-Initiated Development model with the identification of specific steps you can take to improve, depending on your score for each statement or item in the "Know Your Heading" self assessment. In this section you can do intensive analysis and development planning for each of the assessment items. As your coaches, we provide a starting point for the specific development actions you should follow based on your scores. Follow the instructions at the beginning of the "Coaches' Itinerary" to review these specific recommendations.

My Development Plan

This is where you create your personal development plan and build on the information provided in the "Coaches' Itinerary" to determine what actions you are going to take to improve your time management skills and behaviors. You will also identify what resources you may need to accomplish these actions. Finally, assign a realistic date to each action. This is the <u>completion</u> date for each action.

Takeaway Tools

You are provided with three Takeaway Tools to help you improve your skills and behaviors in time management and work-life balance. The first is a checklist of time wasters (Appendix A). This tool will help you realize which time wasters are a problem for you.

The second Takeaway Tool is a template for a meeting agenda (Appendix B). It is important that most meetings have a written agenda to guide the meeting. Use this sample to create your own agenda.

The final Takeaway Tool in Appendix C is a sample Meeting Norming Statement. A norming statement is an agreed-upon statement for how an organization operates. This norming statement can be a baseline for developing your team's meeting guidelines.

Coaches' Bookshelf

If you would like to read further about time management, we have selected a few of the most relevant books to help you. We have also included a brief commentary on each to help guide your reading selection.

4 P's Leadership Competency Model™

Our leadership model is based on 30 skills and behaviors (or competencies) that leaders need to demonstrate to sustain effectiveness and success. We organize the competencies into four areas – Positive Results, Personal Character, People Skills and Persuasive Vision – the 4 P's. To learn more about our Leadership Competency Model, see Appendix E.

Organizational Time Management Improvement

We provide general ideas on how to improve overall time management results at the organizational level using the principles of the SID™ Model.

Summary

We hope the past few pages gave you an idea of how easy this program will be; but, at the same time an appreciation for the methods your coaches will use to walk you through each step and improve your time management skills and behaviors. Our goal is that your time management skills and behaviors are improved by using the Developmental Plan and that you are differentiated from others on your path to success.

"Time = life; therefore, waste your time and waste of your life, or master your time and master your life.."

\- Alan Lakein

Coaches' Questions to Ponder

Have you talked about your time management issues with anyone? If not, why not?

Why do you think effective time management is important to a leader?

What is the relationship between your ability to manage your professional time and your work-life balance?

Coaches Orientation

"I am definitely going to take a course on time management...just as soon as I can work it into my schedule."

- Louis E. Boone

In our coaching practice, regardless of the issues we are discussing with the coachee, time always becomes a topic. Once the subject is broached and we inquire further, it is clear that the coachee has problems managing their time; or, they do not have a healthy work-life balance. We would venture a guess that you have a problem with time management as well. Almost everyone does – including us!

Coach's Comment

When I advise clients to take 20 minutes every other day for "sacred time," time that is devoted to just thinking, they get very unnerved. It is very hard not to do anything but think! With practice, however, they come to relish this time and some even begin to do it every day. Remember, it is not the amount of time spent doing something, it is the quality of the time spent. (Ben)

Importance to an Effective Leader

Almost by definition leaders and managers are very busy. There are many demands of their time and there is always someone to meet with or a project to complete. If a leader is not constantly busy, perhaps they are not doing their job, some may say.

The most effective leaders are very good at managing their time and, as a consequence, are much more productive. Leaders who do not manage their time well are not as happy, not as productive and certainly not as effective. Leaders set the example for using excellent time management skills and behaviors and also in having a good work-life balance.

Think about leaders you have observed that were effective in time management. Did you ever wonder how they managed to get everything done? Were you amazed that they could leave work at a reasonable time and feel they have completed what they set out to accomplish?

Often, it is the organization that is the biggest obstacle for a leader or individual to be effective in time management. Meetings go too long and are not focused on the goals to accomplish. Other departments do not deliver inputs on time. Projects are expected to be completed in an unreasonable timeframe with not enough resources assigned.

Leaders determine whether their organization promotes effective time management or not. Organizations must encourage their employees to practice time management skills and behaviors and, just as important, to strive for a healthy work-life balance. Leaders must set the example in time management and work-life balance.

Time Management and Work-Life Balance Behaviors

Time management behaviors can either be effective or ineffective. The following exercise will focus your thinking on what behaviors are effective and which are ineffective. Consider both time management and work-life balance. Not every behavior is effective for everyone. You will later be asked to consider which are the most effective for you. For now, open your mind and think of all possibilities of time management behaviors and work-life balance.

Exercise

     Using the following chart, list what you think are effective and ineffective time management behaviors.

EFFECTIVE LEADER BEHAVIORS (Time Management)	INEFFECTIVE LEADER BEHAVIORS (Time Management)

The following table shows our response to the previous exercise. You may have listed additional behaviors. Review this list and think about the behaviors you did not include on your list.

EFFECTIVE LEADER BEHAVIORS (Time Management)	INEFFECTIVE LEADER BEHAVIORS (Time Management)
• Prioritizes tasks to ensure important responsibilities are met.	• Does not prioritize tasks to ensure important responsibilities are met.
• Makes the best use of their time.	• Wastes a lot of their own time.
• Makes the best use of others' time.	• Wastes others' time.
• Meets deadlines.	• Typically does not meet deadlines.
• Alters schedule as necessary to address pressing concerns.	• Maintains a strict schedule and is not flexible.
• Manages meeting agendas appropriately.	• Does not keep meetings on topic.
• Manages meetings according to the communicated schedule.	• Does not keep meetings on the communicated schedule.
• Arrives at meetings or events on time.	• Usually late for meetings or events.
• Responds to requests in a timely manner.	• Respond to requests on their time.
• Uses time management tools to streamline productivity.	• Does not concern themselves with time management tools.
• Does not procrastinate and does tasks according to their criticality and importance.	• Puts off tasks, including those that are important or critical to their job or organization.
• Knows how much time is spent on each task.	• Does not know how much time is spent on each task.
• Is organized and ensures that it is easy to find what is needed.	• Disorganized and cannot find documents or items that are needed.
• Deals well with interruptions and keeps them to a minimum.	• Encourages interruptions.

EFFECTIVE LEADER BEHAVIORS (Time Management)	INEFFECTIVE LEADER BEHAVIORS (Time Management)
• Leaves contingency time in schedule to deal with unexpected events or tasks.	• Packs schedule so unexpected events cannot be handled well.
• Says "no" when asked to do tasks outside area of responsibility when appropriate.	• Takes on all tasks when people ask, regardless whether they are in area of responsibility or not.
• Does not allow distractions that interrupt critical work.	• Is often distracted when doing work and creates a distracting environment.
• Delegates time consuming tasks when appropriate.	• Does not delegate time consuming tasks to others when appropriate.
• Engages in exercise or physical activity every day.	• Does not set aside time for exercise or physical activity.
• Sets aside time for planning and scheduling.	• Does not set aside regular time for planning and scheduling.
• "Present in the moment" whether at work or home.	• Mind often wanders when it should be focused on what is at hand.
• Monitors team members to ensure that they are balanced.	• Is not aware of the effort that team members put into tasks.
• Enjoys both work and non-work activities.	• Seems frustrated with both work and non-work activities.

Reflections on Your Behaviors

Think about how much time you waste each day. If you have a serious time management problem or a work-life balance difficulty, we recommend tracking your time in a notebook each day for a week. You may be amazed at how much time is wasted. Doing this will help you see where you can gain some time – time that could be productive or given to your family or non-work life.

Let's Get to the Truth of the Matter

We only have a limited amount of time. In fact, you have less time remaining in your life right now than you did when you began reading this paragraph. Oops – now you have even less time! According to Michael Althsuler, "The bad news is time flies. The good news is you're the pilot." Time is important, very important. Most of us want to spend it wisely, but we think we don't.

Of all the competencies in our leadership model, time management and work-life balance causes the most stress, the most depression, the most divorces, the most estranged relationships. No one is perfect but when we feel we fail at time management or our work-life balance we take it very personal; it is a failure that is evident to those around us, to our family and most importantly to ourselves. Almost everyone feels they can get better at time management and almost everyone desires to have a better work-life balance.

Coach's Comment

Appearances can be deceiving! Have you ever noticed someone who was always busy? You may have assumed that they had a good handle on time management and they were very productive. That may not be the case. Just appearing to be busy does not mean someone is achieving their goals. There are also people who may appear to be very laid back and have excess time on their hands. Your perception may be that they are not productive. In reality, they may have excellent time management skills and are achieving their goals, enabling them to be more laid back. (Sid)

Exercise

What does an ideal day look like to you? Describe it on the next page. What activities would you do to be most productive? List hour-by-hour (or less) what you would like to be doing at work and when you are not at work. On the right side of the page think about yesterday and describe your typical day. Compare the two sides – desired ideal day versus typical day. How much contrast is there? On the following page, ask yourself why there is a disparity. What are the obstacles to achieving your ideal day?

On the following chart, list your ideal activities and typical activities. After completion, compare the two columns.

TIME	IDEAL ACTIVITY	TYPICAL ACTIVITY
1:00 AM		
2:00		
3:00		
4:00		
5:00		
6:00		
7:00		
8:00		
9:00		
10:00		
11:00		

12:00 PM		
1:00		
2:00		
3:00		
4:00		
5:00		
6:00		
7:00		
8:00		
9:00		
10:00		
11:00		
12:00		

Exercise (continued)

Using the information on the previous chart, give some thought and answer these questions:

Why is there a disparity between what you see as your ideal day and your typical day?

What are the obstacles to achieving your ideal day?

In this workbook we will focus on getting alignment between what you desire as your ideal day and the reality of your typical day. We will also provide coaching tips on how to overcome the obstacles that are preventing you from achieving your ideal day.

In addition, we strongly believe in the importance of work-life balance. If your life is balanced you will be better at what you do – whether at work or in your personal life. Being a "workaholic" is a serious disease than needs to be eradicated. Workaholics are not productive, do not have a healthy balance in their life, and lead a dangerous lifestyle. As the saying goes, no one on their deathbed said, "I wish I had spent more time working."

Task Lists

A task list (or a "to-do" list) is a fundamental time management tool. Everyone has a task list. Even those who say they do not, because they don't have their tasks written down, have a task list in their head that they refer to throughout the day.

The most simple task list is one that simply lists the tasks that a person needs to do. When a task is completed it is deleted from the list or checked off in some manner.

TASK	COMPLETED
E-mail Chris about new project requirements	√
Prepare for Unistat meeting	
Complete Luke's performance review	√

Simple Task List

Simple task lists work well for some people, but we recommend using a list that is "tiered," meaning that the tasks are prioritized. To prioritize a task list, either record the tasks in order of highest priority or assign a letter or number to each task. In this example "A" tasks are those that are urgent or important. "B" tasks are those that are important but not urgent and "C" tasks are those that are neither urgent nor important. Theoretically, one should not do B tasks until all the A tasks are completed and B tasks should be completed before any C tasks are tackled. In reality, that approach does not always work. Sometimes the resources needed to complete an A task are not available immediately and a B task is more appropriate.

TASK	PRI	COMPLETED
E-mail Chris about new project requirements	A	√
Prepare for Unistat meeting	A	
Complete Luke's performance review	B	√
Begin next phase of strategic planning	B	
Read Jason's Teledart report	C	

Prioritized Task List

We recommend the prioritized task list so that you stay focused on those tasks that are most important. However, the down side to this type of list is that you usually never get all your tasks completed. The list often grows, resulting in a large number of "C" priority items. We recommend that when that happens you consider delegating some of the C tasks or taking them off the list because they are not important enough to actually be completed. Of course, some C tasks may be promoted to B or A tasks, depending on changing circumstances.

> Don't become a slave to your task list. Use a system that works for you and does not take too much time to maintain.

There are many software applications for creating task lists, some embedded into programs such as the Microsoft Office Suite. Some of these systems can get very elaborate with embedded prioritization, notifications and alarms when tasks are overdue. New applications for tablet PCs are also available. Some people, however, prefer to keep their task list on paper in a notebook. We recommend you try different systems and settle on what works best for you.

How you use your task list must be flexible. Priorities change and new tasks come up all the time. Don't get upset when a changing situation has a direct effect on your tasks.

There is one major danger with task lists – dwelling on managing the list. Your list needs to be functional and able to be maintained quickly. Some people become obsessed with maintaining their lists and the task list becomes a tool for procrastination, therefore directly defeating its purpose. When you prolong the planning activity you are, in fact, procrastinating.

Coaches' Guidance

At a minimum, review your task list daily to refresh your memory about what you need to be doing and to schedule your time. In addition, we recommend reviewing your task list in detail weekly to ensure that all major task are listed and prioritized correctly.

Many people have a lot of responsibility and, consequently, a large task list. A large task list may be appropriate for you, and if you are prioritizing correctly, it won't matter how long the list may be because you are doing the most important tasks first.

Scheduling

Effective scheduling can help you make the best use of your time. Scheduling is the planning to make the best use of your time. As with task lists, scheduling can be simple or it can be more complex. You need to find the system that works for you.

Most people maintain a monthly, weekly and daily schedule. This is important because you need to be able to look ahead to see what events are occurring in the future, preventing you from double booking your time. Scheduling becomes more critical if you are typically involved in a number of meetings or travel frequently.

Again, as with task lists, schedules can be maintained on paper or using a system such as the Microsoft Calendar application. New applications are also available for tablets that enable synchronization across platforms and programs.

We recommend a few tips for effective scheduling

- Be realistic with what you can do with your time. Often, we schedule enough time to complete a task but when interruptions occur or the task becomes more complex, it cannot be completed in time, causing the need to schedule more time to finish what you were doing.

- Always leave open or contingency time in your schedule. We recommend you have contingency time set aside each day, even if only for 30 minutes. This time gives you flexibility and, if not used for an important task, becomes a gift to enable you to do lesser priority tasks.

- At the beginning of each week, and each day for that matter, seriously consider your schedule in conjunction with your task list and priorities. Be sure that you have your highest priority tasks scheduled and with enough time to do the best job possible. Again, as you review your schedule, ensure that you have contingency time built in as blocked time.

Scheduling is a five-step process:

1. Identify the time you have available (block out personal time, regularly scheduled meetings, and appointments).

2. Block in the essential tasks you must do to succeed (urgent, high priority tasks)
3. Schedule vital housekeeping tasks such as customer responses, performance reviews, notes from meetings, etc.
4. Block in contingency time to handle unpredicted interruptions.
5. Schedule activities that address your personal priorities and development.

Coaches' Guidance

Do not over commit yourself by filling in all time on your schedule. If your day is filled with wall-to-wall meetings, when do you get your work done? Seriously consider all entries into your task list and schedule and be sure to include the time to get your work completed.

Discipline

Time management tools are excellent - but they are just that - tools. What gives someone effective management over their time is discipline. Schedules and task lists are fine, but only if they are used and managed well. If not, they only serve to consume time.

If you have difficulty disciplining yourself to effectively manage your time through a task list and schedule, we recommend an accountability partner to help monitor your time management behaviors. Your partner can review your task list and schedule, and ensure that you follow them.

An accountability partner can also help you avoid time wasters, which we will cover next. Having someone call out your time wasting behaviors will motivate you to improve.

It is important to understand the difference between being busy and being productive. Being busy is not important – yes, it may impress some people in the short term, but being productive is what matters. Having a full schedule is not necessarily being productive; although it gives the appearance of being busy. For example, busy people answer e-mails immediately (all of them); productive people answer e-mails promptly according to their importance and they make time in their schedule to determine the importance of each. Busy people complicate things; productive people try hard to keep everything simple. Busy people try to take care of everything; productive people take care of what is important and delegate if possible.

Time Wasters

The biggest problem that people have in managing time are "time wasters." The following are some of the biggest time wasters and some simple steps to combat each.

Meetings

Unfortunately, meetings are necessary. However, many meetings are poorly managed and as a result are not as productive as needed. Because meetings involve multiple people, the time wasted is multiplied to become an expensive proposition. Often, time is wasted in a meeting when people are late or the meeting goes off the agenda.

Antidote: All meetings should have a published agenda. All meetings should start on time, regardless if all attendees are present. The meeting should be managed by someone who can keep the meeting on track and finished at the scheduled time. Action items should be captured and assigned. Issues that arise during the meeting that are not on the agenda should be listed on a "parking lot" and addressed outside the meeting or at another session when the topic is on the agenda. As a leader, it is your responsibility to instill meeting management skills across the organization.

Interruptions

Interruptions not only steal time from you but, more important, break your concentration from what you are focusing on at the time. Interruptions occur because we allow them to happen. This can be a major problem for leaders who feel they should have an "open door" and people can visit them at any time.

Antidote: When working on anything that requires concentration, close your door and put a do not disturb sign. Include a time when you will be available. If you do not have a door to your work area, find a place to put a do not disturb sign to prevent people from arbitrarily interrupting you. If you want to have an open door policy for people to drop in to discuss issues, establish a time each day for this to occur. People will respect your time if they know they can talk with you during that time.

Distractions

There are many different types of distractions – noise in the office, pending deadlines, worry, lack of clarity on tasks, and so on. All of these distractions effect your concentration on the task at hand.

Antidote: Do what you can do to eliminate distractions. For example, if there is a lot of noise around you, wear noise-cancelling headphones either with relaxing music or no music playing. Develop your skills in compartmentalizing your thoughts. In other words, try to only think about the task at hand when you are trying to focus. Set aside time after you are finished to think about what else needs to be done or issues you need to consider.

Social Media

Social media sites such as Facebook, Twitter and LinkedIn can become tremendous distractions throughout the day. It is easy to "pop in" and see what is happening with friends and colleagues around the world. This serves as a distraction from what you should be concentrating on at the time.

Antidote: Monitor your time on social media sites. Most likely you are spending too much time on these sites when you should be working or concentrating on your tasks. Put the social media sites "off limits" when you are working. Catch up on them during breaks or after you have completed your tasks for the day. Just as with any bad habit, it may be hard to do this for a while but it is critical. Social media sites can consume you and cause you to be very ineffective in managing your time.

Internet

The Internet has given us great capabilities, particularly when needing new information. The vast amount of information can turn a simple hunt for a quote or information about a client into a long session that goes far astray. It also gives the capability of integrating our personal and professional lives. For example, you decide while working to go to a movie that evening. Your next step may be to go online to get tickets, make restaurant reservations, read reviews about the movie, get directions to the theater. Before you know it, a half hour is gone and you've gotten nothing done.

Antidote: Unless necessary for the task at hand, do not use the Internet until you take a break. Some people do well scheduling time at lunch to use the

Internet for personal reasons. Others discipline themselves to only use the Internet for personal reasons when they are at home. However you manage yourself in this area, do it now and set the rules. Otherwise, you may waste hours each day from being productive.

E-mail

E-mail has become a necessary evil in how we communicate at work and in our personal life. Some people literally spend all day at their computer working e-mails…their job has become totally e-mail driven. Think of how many times each day you check your mail. Think how much time you spend responding to e-mails.

Antidote: Develop an e-mail protocol. For example, one rule could be that you only check e-mail three times per day. Another would be that you turn off e-mail while you are working on a project or task. Establish rules about what e-mails you will respond to and which you will not. (For example, an e-mail asking a simple yes or no question can turn into a long string that takes 15 minutes to complete.) Tell your colleagues and direct reports what your e-mail policy is and adhere to it. Encourage others to adopt their own e-mail rules.

The Pomodoro Technique

In the late 1980's, Francesco Cirillo came up with a unique method to improve time management skills and productivity. He named it The Pomodoro Technique, after the Italian name for a tomato. Why a tomato? His technique is based on using a kitchen timer to measure time spent working and the timer he had available at the time was in the likeness of a tomato. His technique caught on and is very popular.

The Pomodoro Technique is built on 30 minute increments (25 minutes work and 5 minutes break). It is broken into these segments of time because research shows we are most efficient and attentive in 25-minute increments. The unit of measure is, of course, called a pomodoro. At the beginning of the day you review your task list (in priority order) and assign a number of pomodoros to each task. For example, in writing this section of the workbook I assigned myself one pomodoro.

The next step is to set the timer for 25 minutes. Once the timer begins, start working and do not stop until the timer rings. Do everything you can to minimize interruptions. If you are interrupted for a few seconds, simply continue working without resetting the pomodoro. If, however, the interruption is longer than a few seconds, you must begin again by resetting the pomodoro.

When the pomodoro is completed (the timer rings), take a break whether you are finished with the task or not. After a 5-minute break, begin a new pomodoro and continue. After four pomodoros, you are entitled to a longer break – at least fifteen minutes. This time could also be used for lunch, a quick walk or time to do another activity you enjoy.

If you complete a task before the current pomodoro is finished, do not move to another task. Use the gained time to improve on what you have done. For instance, I set my pomodoro when beginning to write this section. I finished with 10:26 remaining on my pomodoro. This gives me time to go back and reread the section, add some additional content and also add the book to the Coaches' Bookshelf in the appendix.

There is a bit more complexity involved regarding interruptions, tracking pomodoro's and analysis, but this is the fundamental premise of Cirillo's method. His book, the Pomodoro Technique, can be downloaded in PDF format free at http://www.pomodorotechnique.com. You will also find other time management resources related to the Pomodoro Technique, including kitchen timers that look like Italian tomatoes! For those with iPads and iPhones, there are pomodoro applications that can be used for your task list and timer.

We recommend you scan Cirillo's book and give the Pomodoro Technique an opportunity to see if it works for you. We have found that it not only gives us good work increments with breaks to "re-energize" but also improves focus on the task at hand – the gentle clicking of the timer reminds us we should be focusing on our work.

Procrastination

One of the best ways to avoid doing a difficult task is to find something else to do. Many of us do very well at procrastination. All we need to do is go to our task list and find something else that needs to be done and BINGO! we have found a way to avoid what we don't want to do – and we have justified it because the task we are now doing is something from our task list.

Overcoming procrastination can be very, very difficult, especially if a person has become very good at it over the years. The best approach to solving procrastination is to review the task list each morning and firmly decide what is going to be worked on that day. Then, review the list with an accountability partner who will challenge your decision if there are missing tasks. If you use the accountability partner regularly they will be able to detect when you are avoiding a difficult task and challenge you.

Laura Spencer, in a freelance blog, identified the 10 top tips to combat procrastination. We tend to agree with her thinking and urge you to consider them since procrastination can be a career stopper – especially for those who work for themselves.

1. Set a schedule
2. Get organized
3. Find an accountability partner
4. Break large tasks into smaller ones
5. Don't over commit
6. Control distractions
7. Figure out what motivates you
8. Track your progress
9. Tackle self-doubt and other psychological issues
10. Reward your success

Work-Life Balance

Time management and work-life balance are very inter-related. If you get more done in less time at your work, you will have more time to devote to your personal life. Many people have difficulty finding the right balance. Often, because of priorities on either side, life is unbalanced. The goal should be to try to consistently keep as close to being balanced as possible. A good work-life balance varies from person-to-person and only you know what the best balance is for you, your family and your work situation.

Being out of balance goes both ways. If you are out of balance because you are working too much – taking work home, working on weekends, working late, and not being able to disengage – your personal life will suffer. Likewise, if you do not give what is expected to your job because it always takes a backseat to your personal interests, your professional life will suffer.

Your professional life is important; but your personal health and life are more important. Being healthy and having a good balance between your professional and personal life helps make you more productive in both. Effective leaders learn how to achieve balance and monitor when it becomes unbalanced and take action to bring it back to where they are most comfortable. Here are some tips for achieving and maintaining work-life balance:

- Be effective in time management so that you can get the most done during your work time.

- Compartmentalize your thinking so you are "present in the moment" whether you are at work or at home.

- Engage in physical activities that will give you energy and focus.

- Have an attitude of continuous learning, whether related to your professional life or an outside activity.

- Have a trusted colleague serve as your accountability partner. This person will detect when you are out of balance and help you recover.

> ### *Coaches' Guidance*
>
> *Have you ever heard the phrase, "Stop and smell the roses?" Do you? I love vacations and one reason is that I have the time to stop and smell the roses – or in my case, watch a beautiful sunset from a beach with my wife. We could sit there for hours and not say a word, but it is the most treasured time we spend. But, I learned that you don't have to go on vacation to smell the roses. Take in everyday life. Sit on your back porch and listen to the birds. Walk a quiet path through the woods and find a place to sit and just listen. Smell the roses every day. (Ben)*

Map Your Growth

Time Management is related to a number of other competencies in our 4P's Competency Model™. It is important to understand the relationship between time management and the related competencies. For example, if scheduling or prioritizing are weaknesses for you, creating a culture in your organization that is time-management focused will be more difficult.

On the next page we show the most relevant leadership competencies within our 4P's Competency Model™ to time management, and beginning on the next page, is a chart for you to complete to describe the relationship between each competency and time management. For example, what impact does this competency have on your time management behaviors? There is no "right" or "wrong" answer. Our description of the relationships begins on page 57.

4P's Competency Model™
Time Management Related Competencies

Persuasive Vision

Inspiration
Planning
Strategic Thinking

People Skills

Interpersonal Skills
Problem Solving
Talent Management

Positive Results

Commitment to Quality
Focus on Results

Personal Character

Credibility
Followership
Initiative
Stress Management

COMPETENCY	RELATIONSHIP TO TIME MANAGEMENT

Persuasive Vision

Inspiration	
Planning	
Strategic Thinking	

Positive Results

Commitment to Quality	
Focus on Results	

COMPETENCY	RELATIONSHIP TO TIME MANAGEMENT

*Personal
Character*

Credibility	
Followership	
Initiative	
Stress Management	

People Skills

Interpersonal Skills	
Problem Solving	
Talent Management	

COMPETENCY	RELATIONSHIP TO TIME MANAGEMENT

Persuasive Vision

Inspiration	Leaders who manage their time well and have an excellent work-life balance are inspirational to others.
Planning	Successful time management requires planning skills. In addition, having time available to plan increases the opportunities for success.
Strategic Thinking	Effective time management allows the leader time to devote to strategic thinking.

Positive Results

Commitment to Quality	Quality takes time and if you are effective at time management you will devote more of your resources to creating quality in your products or services.
Focus on Results	Some leaders will appear to be very busy and results-oriented but they are not effective. Instead they are focused on so much to do they are not able to pay attention and focus on achieving the results they want.

COMPETENCY	RELATIONSHIP TO TIME MANAGEMENT

Personal Character

Credibility	A leader who is effective at time management establishes credibility by having the time to "do things right."
Followership	A good follower manages time well and gets the tasks done that are important to senior leadership and the organization.
Initiative	Effective time managers will have the time available to demonstrate their initiative and will be effective in achieving the goals of each effort in the shortest amount of time.
Stress Management	Leaders who are effective at time management demonstrate less stress because they have the time to do what needs to be done and still maintain a healthy work-life balance.

People Skills

Interpersonal Skills	Leaders who are effective with managing their time are easier to get along with and have the time to build personal and professional relationships.
Problem Solving	It takes time to solve problems. Effective time management gives the leader the time to consider the alternatives and systematically deal with problems.
Talent Management	Leading and managing employees takes time. Effective time managers set aside time to take care of their staff, whether it is coaching, feedback or relationship building.

The Daily Journey

Every organization should strive to ensure that their employees are given the tools to be effective at time management. Consider the following case study:

Mr. Perfect?

Josh was so well organized some people actually made fun of him; with respect of course. Actually, most of his colleagues admired him and wondered how he could get everything done that was on his plate.

His work life revolved around his "to-do" list. He kept a copy with him at all times and referred to it frequently throughout the day. It wasn't anything fancy – a simple piece of paper with the tasks listed that he planned to work on that day. He made the list each evening for the next day's activities. He could look at this schedule and see which meetings he had coming up and plan his time around his obligations.

Josh was never late for a meeting and was always prepared. He insisted on an agenda and ensured that it was followed. When he held a meeting of his staff it was usually a "stand up" meeting that lasted no more than 15 minutes and followed a standard agenda.

Most people quickly realized that Josh only checked e-mail twice a day during a scheduled time – first thing in the morning and right after lunch. He responded to e-mails when necessary and filed informational e-mails in a specific folder on his computer. He had strict rules about e-mail: If the sender expected him to take action the mail would be addressed to him and it needed to be specified when the action needed completion. If the e-mail was informational the sender needed to only "cc" him.

His office was a model of organization. He knew where everything was located and if he needed a document it could be produced in seconds. Josh did not tolerate interruptions unless it was an emergency. He was polite, but firm, when admonishing those who interrupted him without a valid reason.

On top of his work responsibilities, Josh also coached his son's soccer team, participated in church activities and almost 100% of the time was out the door at 5:00 to meet his wife for a tennis match on the way home. When he needed to work late, which was rare, he became ultra-focused and finished his tasks as quickly as possible.

GIVE US YOUR THOUGHTS!

- Do you think Josh was always so organized and thoughtful in how he did things?

- How do you think Josh's focus impacted others on his team?

- How did Josh's rules about meetings help or hinder the organization?

- Do you think Josh had a good work-life balance? If so, how did that help him in his everyday work?

- Do you think Josh's rules around e-mail helped or hurt him?

For our thoughts on the questions about this case study, turn to the next page. Our thoughts are not necessarily the "right answers." Your responses on the previous page may be excellent and add an additional perspective on the questions. The important thing is that you think each question through and give your best response.

Coaches' Questions to Ponder

Is your behavior or that of someone you know similar to Josh's in this example? If so, how did it affect you?

OUR THOUGHTS

- Do you think Josh was always so organized and thoughtful in how he did things?

  Possibly, but more than likely Josh adopted these behaviors over time because he could see the negative effects of poor time management and work-life balance. Most of us begin our career with little control or discipline over how we work. We adopt improvements to our work style by learning and observing others who do it well.

- How do you think Josh's focus impacted others on his team?

  Most were likely envious and wished they could be as organized as Josh. Some may have mocked his style but they probably envied him when they needed to work longer hours to get things done. As a leader, Josh should focus on mentoring others in his work habits so that others could improve their time management and work-life balance.

- How did Josh's rules about meetings help or hinder the organization?

  Very likely they helped the organization. Most of us would agree that our organization has too many meetings and the ones that take place are poorly organized and take twice as much time as needed. Josh wasn't averse to meeting, but did require that they have a purpose, an agenda, and an appropriate timeframe. He also insisted that the meetings stay on track and not divert to other topics. These "rules" helped the organization by giving people more time to work on their projects and less time spent in long, meaningless meetings.

- Do you think Josh had a good work-life balance? If so, how did that help him in his everyday work?

  It appears that he did have a good work-life balance. He was able to spend time with his family daily and was able to leave work at a reasonable time. He had outside activities that gave him a release from the rigors of his job. Most likely this enabled him to focus "in the moment" whether he was at work or with his family.

- Do you think Josh's rules around e-mail helped or hurt him?

  Many people are trapped by e-mail and their work life revolves around sending and receiving e-mails throughout the day. Josh's rules helped him to focus on e-mail when appropriate and focus on other things the rest of the time. One thing that helps when establishing an e-mail schedule is to let others know when you will be checking e-mail and responding. He made it clear that if he needed to respond or take action he would do so if the mail was addressed to him, but the response would need to wait until the next scheduled e-mail time. If Josh is in a critical position, it may help if he had a pager or a special number to be reached at in case of an emergency.

To improve, it is good to analyze examples of poor time management skills and behaviors. Consider the following case study:

Procrastinatus Interruptus!

Amy had a simple way of prioritizing her tasks – whatever was the easiest got her attention immediately. She hated doing things that were difficult and always procrastinated until the last minute to do them. Then, because she didn't have much time to complete them, these tasks were always done with poor quality. Amy was noted for the mistakes she made in documents.

She was also noted for always being late to meetings. This even happened when she was the person calling the meeting! Her meetings never ended as scheduled, always running over because she tried to accomplish many things beyond the scope of the meeting.

People were very frustrated with Amy for two other reasons. First, she often interrupted people when they were busy. She would simply barge into an office and begin talking with a person about her troubles, many of the conversations being about her failing marriage. She also sent out hundreds of e-mails a day, many just asking one or two simple question, but with long, drawn-out explanations. If people didn't respond to her immediately she fired off a "zinger" repudiating the person for not responding fast enough.

Amy often worked late into the evening, although others that observed her after hours thought that she was just keeping busy and not really accomplishing much.

Amy's boss, Justine, talked with her regularly about these issues. Amy's excuse was always that she had too much to do and was always short on time because of her workload. She always bemoaned her peers for not being responsive and giving her the information she needed in time. When Justine asked to review her "to-do" list, Amy stated that her list was in her head and not on paper. She didn't maintain a calendar, let alone a prioritized list of tasks. When Justine confronted her about her meeting behaviors, Amy responded by saying that meetings were the only time she could get everyone together to give her the information she needed. Her excuse for being late for meetings was that she was busy preparing for the meeting and always lot track of time.

Justine had no choice but to put Amy on probation. Even though she respected Amy's talents, she was a great disruption to the others in the office and was always late completing projects that were of poor quality; certainly not up to the standards the company demanded.

GIVE US YOUR THOUGHTS!

- Why do you think Amy focused on getting the easy tasks completed first?

- What could Amy have done instead of interrupting others to talk about her problems?

- How did Amy's being late for meetings affect other people?

- Do you think Amy created much of her own stress?

- Do you think there was a connection between Amy's work habits and her problems at home?

- Do you think Justine's action in putting Amy on probation was too harsh?

- What steps should Justine recommend to Amy to improve during her probation period?

For our thoughts on the questions about this case study, turn to the next page. Our thoughts are not necessarily the "right answers." Your responses on the previous page may be excellent and add an additional perspective on the questions. The important thing is that you think each question through and give your best response.

Coaches' Questions to Ponder

Is your behavior or that of someone you know similar to Amy's? If so, how did it affect you?

OUR THOUGHTS

- Why do you think Amy focused on getting the easy tasks completed first?

  Simple – they were easy tasks to do and it made her feel like she was accomplishing something without putting in too much effort. She could congratulate herself at the end of the day, saying she got a lot of tasks finished; but, the major, important tasks were left undone.

- What could Amy have done instead of interrupting others to talk about her problems?

  She should have been respectful of others' time and their focus on work. She should have talked with someone she trusted during her off-duty time. Her personal problems should not have been brought into the workplace.

- How did Amy's being late for meetings affect other people?

  Peoples' time is important and most likely they became very frustrated with her behaviors. In addition, some people would model her behavior and be late themselves, developing bad habits. Extending meetings beyond the scheduled time is also inconsiderate. Not only is it an infringement on others' time but most likely they would not be prepared to discuss the additional topics she brought up.

- Do you think Amy created much of her own stress?

  Yes, Amy's work style can be very stressful. In her mind she knows that she is not working to her potential and is not producing quality work. This stress feeds upon itself when she doesn't get things done, has troubles at home and is reprimanded by her boss.

- Do you think there was a connection between Amy's work habits and her problems at home?

  Most likely Amy's behavior is directly related with her problems at home. Her work style and stress from work very well may have contributed to her failing marriage. Consequently she put in extra time, avoiding time at home and at the same time feeling she was accomplishing something at work.

- Do you think Justine's action in putting Amy on probation was too harsh?

  No, eventually leaders must address people with work habits like Amy's. If not, it affects productivity of the entire work unit.

- What steps should Justine recommend to Amy to improve during her probation period?

  Justine should recommend that Amy improve her time management skills, learn how to deal with her stress, and assign her a mentor to work with her on her time and quality issues.

What Would You Do?

Instructions

The following are examples of poor time management behaviors. After each behavior, describe how to change or fix the behaviors.

1. "Checking in" on Facebook periodically during the day.

2. Delaying completion of difficult, important tasks until the last moment.

3. Keeping your "to-do" list in your head as you go through the day.

4. Sending repeated e-mails, essentially having a conversation, with someone within walking distance.

5. Having to work late almost every day in order to get the minimum requirements of the job completed.

6. Getting into the routine of taking work home every day.

7. Working every Saturday (or other day off) to catch up on projects or e-mails.

8. Never seeming to be able to make the "to-do" list smaller; rather, having it grow each day until you determine you must work the weekend to catch up.

9. Spending time with the family, but thinking about work problems as you do so.

Exercise

Add any examples of poor time management skills and behaviors that you have experienced.

Your Coaches' Thoughts

The following are our thoughts about each of these poor time management skills and behaviors. Compare them to your thoughts on the previous pages.

1.   "Checking in" on Facebook periodically during the day.

     Facebook and other social media sites should not be part of your routine during work time. If important, check these sites during lunch or a scheduled break time. Do not use the need to check these sites as an excuse to take a break.

2.   Delaying completion of difficult, important tasks until the last moment.

     You should not avoid difficult, important tasks; in fact, these should be your priority. If you take the time to plan each week and each day, you are more apt to give the time to important projects that is needed. When you prioritize your tasks you know where your focus should be and you become more productive when the important tasks are out of the way.

3.   Keeping your "to-do" list in your head as you go through the day.

     A list of tasks to be completed should be on paper or in an electronic tool to enable easy reference and prioritization. We can't possibly remember everything that needs to be done by keeping it in our head. A "to-do" list is a living document that shows the priority of each task (and deadline if applicable).

4.   Sending repeated e-mails, essentially having a conversation, with someone within walking distance.

     If you need to have a conversation with someone nearby, get up, go to them and see if they are available. If not available at the moment, schedule a time to talk. If you only require a simple answer, then an e-mail is fine, but once you have the answer do not continue the e-mail string.

5.   Having to work late almost every day in order to get the minimum requirements of the job completed.

     You should be able to do your work during normal hours except on rare occasions. If you cannot get your work done during normal hours over a long period of time, evaluate if you are being productive during that time. If you are being productive and simply have too much work for one person, you have a responsibility to bring it to the attention of your manager or leader. Also, ask yourself if you are working late to avoid other problems, such as those at home.

6. Getting into the routine of taking work home every day.

   It is very easy to take work home and rationalize that you are more productive at home than in the workplace. But, are you taking work home because you are not productive at work? Or, are you taking work home to avoid conflict or other negative situations at home? Do your best to leave your work at the workplace and focus on your family and other interests during your off time.

7. Working every Saturday (or other day off) to catch up on projects or e-mails.

   Again, this displays a poor work-life balance and poor time management skills. If you need to work during your off time on a normal basis to catch up, whether on projects or e-mail, you are not scheduling your time right during normal work hours. Your time off should be a time of relaxation, family responsibilities and doing things you enjoy. This should refresh you and energize you to get things done during normal work time.

8. Never seeming to be able to make the "to-do" list smaller; rather, having it grow each day until you determine you must work the weekend to catch up.

   Some people thrive on making the longest to-do list possible and then never being able to complete their tasks. They become slaves to the ever-growing list. Do your best to make up a list at the end of each day to govern your work for the following day. Don't add things as you go. Focus on taking things off the list, not putting them on.

9. Spending time with the family, but thinking about work problems as you do so.

   Learn to "be in the moment." When you are off duty, do your best not to think about work. Focus on your leisure activities and clear your mind of the problems you face most of the week. Likewise, when you are at work, focus on what needs to be done, not what you are going to be doing during your off time. Being "in the moment" makes us better at what we are doing at the moment.

Know Your Heading

Now that you have a better understanding of time management and its associated behaviors, it is time to self assess your current behaviors. To focus your future development activities and achieve your goals, it is important that you be reflective and honest in completing your self assessment. As you reflect on each statement, consider how others would respond as well. Think about how others perceive your behavior related to each statement.

Instructions: Read each of the skills and behaviors below. As objectively as possible, score yourself for each according to the following scale: 1 = strongly disagree; 2 = disagree; 3 = agree; 4 = strongly agree. If a behavior is not appropriate for your position or aspired position, check the N/A column.

The PG column indicates the page number for a deeper discussion of development recommendations for each behavioral statement based on your score. Later you will refer to these pages to help you complete your development action plan.

SKILL OR BEHAVIOR	1 (SD)	2 (D)	3 (A)	4 (SA)	N/A	PG
I alter my schedule as necessary to address pressing concerns.						80
I manage meeting agendas appropriately.						84
I make the best use of my time.						88
I make the best use of others' time.						92
I manage meetings according to the communicated schedule.						96
I meet deadlines.						100
I prioritize my tasks to insure that important responsibilities are fulfilled.						104

SKILL OR BEHAVIOR	1 (SD)	2 (D)	3 (A)	4 (SA)	N/A	PG
I respond in a timely manner to requests.						108
I use time management techniques and tools to streamline efficiency and productivity.						112
I always arrive at meetings or events on time.						116
I do tasks according to their criticality and importance without procrastinating.						120
I know how much time I spend on various jobs.						124
I am organized and it is easy for me to find what I need.						128
I manage interruptions well and keep them at a minimum.						132
I leave contingency time in my schedule to deal with "the unexpected."						136
I say "no" when asked to do tasks that are not in my area of responsibility when appropriate.						140
I do not get distracted from tasks I am working on.						144
I delegate time-consuming tasks when appropriate.						148
I use goals, plans and measures to guide my efforts.						152
I do not "make work."						156
I use a manageable to-do list focusing on what needs to be done.						160
I engage in physical activity every day.						164
I only work outside normal hours when necessary.						168

SKILL OR BEHAVIOR	1 (SD)	2 (D)	3 (A)	4 (SA)	N/A	PG
I set aside time for planning and scheduling.						172
I reward myself after an achievement.						176
I am "present in the moment" whether at work or not at work.						180
I monitor team members to ensure that they have balance.						184
I enjoy both work and non-work activities.						188
I coach colleagues and direct reports who have time management issues.						192

Scoring

Review your score for each item. Based on your score for an item, follow the directions below:

- Read the Coaches' Guidance beginning on the next page. Regardless of your score, this section will provide valuable tips to improve your time management skills and behaviors.

- For each item, especially those in which you scored a (1) strongly disagree or (2) disagree, refer to the development recommendations page in the Coaches' Itinerary section for that item. Read and consider the recommendations for that item.

Coaches' Guidance

Coaches' Comment

Time management is your friend! Take steps to get your time under control. Not every day can be maximum efficiency but you know that you can do better.

As your coaches for this competency, we recommend reading the tips provided below. From our coaching experience, taking heed of this information will be a good step toward developing this competency. For additional guidance and specific recommendations based on your self-assessment score, see the developmental resources in the next section of this workbook. Time management and work-life balance are critical to your success and the success of your team.

- **Strive to make the best use of your time**. You are in control of your time. If it is out of control and you are wasting time or not balancing it well, you are the one who must take action. Yes, there may be times you are required to do something that you feel is not the best use of your time, but rarely. You control how you allocate your time across your tasks.

- **Be aware of how you use others' time**. Be conscious of how you are interacting with others. Meet deadlines so others can meet theirs. Don't spend inordinate amounts of time socializing with others during work; it consumes their time as well as yours.

- **Especially focus on how you can improve meeting management as a time saver**. Always have an agenda for meetings – and if it is your meeting, you are responsible for this. Ensure that all meetings start on time and stay on the agenda. As a leader, you know if meetings are a problem in your organization. If so, take responsibility for creating a better meeting culture – one that minimizes time and achieves results.

- **Be aware of time wasters and actively seek to eliminate them**. Limit your time on e-mail and social media sites. Set up clear personal e-mail rules and adhere to them. Examine how you waste time and take immediate steps to eliminate the behaviors that are consuming your time. Minutes add up so don't excuse yourself by saying you are doing something only for a few minutes each hour.

- **Adopt time management tools such as a task list and schedule to control your time**. Learn to use these basic tools to your advantage. Your task list should not only identify what you need to do but also show the priority of each task. Manage your schedule for each week and each day; but, be flexible because things happen each day to impact your schedule. Your task list and schedule are tools to use in managing your time but you should not become obsessed with them; use them, but don't abuse them.

- **Prioritize your tasks**. Each day you should prioritize your tasks so you work on the most important jobs at hand. Often, the priority of your work comes from someone else. Respect that and assign the right priority for each task. Don't assign a high priority to a task just because it is easy or something you enjoy doing.

- **Don't procrastinate**. The work you choose to do should be based on need and criticality. Do the hard work or complex work first if they are in your high priority list. It is easy to rationalize that you can get more enjoyable, smaller tasks completed faster, giving you more time to do the difficult work. It doesn't usually work that way. If you are in the habit of procrastinating, you will rarely get the hard work completed.

- **Strive to get your work done during normal hours**. It is great to be loyal and work hard, but you need a life outside work, if only to energize you to be better when you are working. Sometimes you may need to work outside normal hours, but it should never be the routine. If you are managing your time well throughout the day you should not normally need to take work home or stay late. Do NOT engage in "face time" – staying extra hours at work, even if there is nothing to do, just to look good to your boss.

- **Be aware of your work-life balance**. You should have a good work-life balance for many reasons – health, relationships and efficiency at work are some very good reasons. If you are out of balance, think how you can scale back your work so you can focus on your personal life. Do you need to delegate more? Are you avoiding problems in your personal life? Neglecting to take care of your work-life balance will quickly lead to problems. Creating boundaries between your work and personal life is just as important as learning how to transition between them.

- **Set aside time to manage your task list and schedule**. Most people devote time to do this in the morning. Make any changes that are necessary and then do your best to focus on your priority tasks and stay on your schedule. It only takes a few minutes and will keep you at top efficiency throughout the day.

- **Monitor the time management and work-life balance of your colleagues and team members**. As a leader you have a responsibility to ensure that your colleagues and team members have a good work-life balance. If not, talk with them and help them improve. A happy team that works at peak efficiency is much more productive than one that exhibits constant stress because it is out of balance.

"It's not enough to be busy, so are the ants. The question is, what are we busy about?"

- Henry David Thoreau

Coaches' Questions to Ponder

Are you ready to concentrate intently on improving your time management skills and behaviors?

How much time do you have available each week to devote to professional improvement?

Are you satisfied with the scores you gave yourself on the "Know Your Heading" self assessment?

Part 3 – Development Recommendations

Coaches' Itinerary

In this section you can do intensive analysis and development planning for each of the items in the "Know Your Heading" self assessment for Time Management. Although we encourage you to read all items and their recommendations, we urge you to specifically focus on those items that you scored yourself a 1 (strongly disagree) or 2 (disagree) and create a development plan based on the recommendations for those items. We also urge that you review the recommendations for items that you scored a 3 (agree) or 4 (strongly agree) and learn more how you can emphasize a strength or work toward creating a culture of effective time management in your organization.

Each item also has an introductory page with Your Coaches' Comments about the Item. Reach each comment as well. Your Coaches also have provided a challenge for each item. Read and consider the questions or directions in the challenge.

I alter my schedule as necessary to address pressing concerns.

Wouldn't it be wonderful if every day went as planned? Unfortunately, this is rarely the case. Leaders must be flexible and open to altering their schedule when pressing concerns arise. This should be done without undue concern or negative comment. Rather, the effective leader takes the changes in stride and focuses on the pressing concern until it is resolved. Then, a quick revision of the schedule can get the leader back on track.

Coaches' Challenge

Have you ever noticed people who could not adapt well to a change in their schedule? What kind of behaviors did they exhibit to express their displeasure? Are these behaviors that leaders should demonstrate, particularly in front of their peers and direct reports?

On the next two pages, circle the score you gave yourself for this statement in the "Know Your Heading" exercise. Then, read the Coaches' Recommendations for your score.

"If you want to make good use of your time,
You've got to know what's most important and then give it all you've got."
- Lee Iacocca

I alter my schedule as necessary to address pressing concerns.

Your Score: 1 (strongly disagree) 2 (disagree) 3 (agree) 4 (strongly agree)

Score: 1	Coaches' Recommendations

Apparently you do not feel you are flexible and get distraught when you need to alter your schedule. We recommend that you first understand that pressing concerns are important and happen all the time; and as a leader you must adapt. Second, when this occurs, take the time immediately to rework your schedule to accommodate the pressing concern.

Be careful not to demonstrate your frustration or anger to your peers or direct reports. They will often mimic your behavior and make a difficult situation even worse. As a leader you need to *lead* the reaction that people have when faced with a schedule change. Understand that schedule changes can occur frequently and your challenge is to rework your schedule to minimize the impact on those activities that are important to you as well as the organization.

Score: 2	Coaches' Recommendations

You see a need to improve in this area. If you dislike changes to your schedule, focus on how you can adapt better to changes. Remember, the change is typically done for good reasons (the pressing concern) and may very well be outside your control. Thus, you have a choice and that choice is in how you react to the change. We recommend that at your first opportunity you rework your schedule so that the pressing concern you face does not have a major impact on your other tasks. Perhaps you will have to reschedule some "nice to-do" tasks to a later date.

As a leader, you control your reaction to changes in your schedule. Consider your normal reactions to changes. How could you react more positive so that others follow your lead?

I alter my schedule as necessary to address pressing concerns.

Your Score: 1 (strongly disagree) 2 (disagree) 3 (agree) 4 (strongly agree)

Score: 3	Coaches' Recommendations

This is a good score and you feel that you normally do not have a problem in altering your schedule when needing to address other important issues. Continue to take this approach and focus on how you can minimize the impact on your other tasks that need to be delayed. Is there anyone you need to notify of the schedule change? As a leader you need to be sure that all important tasks are done as scheduled. If there is a change, you may need to alter completion of some tasks and notify others as needed.

Observe your peers and how they react to making schedule changes. If it gives them stress, talk to them and give them some pointers on how they can react better, especially when being observed by their direct reports.

Score: 4	Coaches' Recommendations

This is an excellent score and demonstrates that you recognize that sometimes pressing concerns and impromptu events take place that require altering your schedule. As a leader you should observe your peers and direct reports and provide feedback to them regarding how they react to changes in their schedule.

Changing your schedule should have minimal impact on getting other tasks completed if you have planned your activities well. Certainly, some impacts have more of an effect than others, such as an unscheduled trip that must occur. However, the effective leader can review their schedule, delegate as necessary and figure out a way to get their needs accomplished.

I alter my schedule as necessary to address pressing concerns.

List the development steps you will take to improve in this item.

1.

2.

3.

4.

Other Notes:

I manage meeting agendas appropriately.

This is a major complaint we get when coaching or consulting with organizations. Most meetings are poorly managed and allowed to drift from the agenda too easily and without cause. This, of course, assumes that the meeting has a printed and communicated agenda (many do not). Meetings cost money – often a lot of money. That is why every meeting should be managed well and flow according to a well thought out agenda.

Coaches' Challenge

Think about meetings you have been in that have been poorly managed. How did you feel during the meeting? Most likely you felt like it was a waste of your time. What about meetings you call and are leading? Do you always have an agenda?

On the next two pages, circle the score you gave yourself for this statement in the "Know Your Heading" exercise. Then, read the Coaches' Recommendations for your score.

"To get something done a committee should consist of no more than three people, two of whom are absent."
- Robert Copeland

I manage meeting agendas appropriately.

Your Score: 1 (strongly disagree) 2 (disagree) 3 (agree) 4 (strongly agree)

Score: 1	Coaches' Recommendations

We appreciate your candor in answering this question. If your problem is that you do not produce a written agenda for your meetings, start to do so now. Why is this important? If you are inviting people to attend the meeting you have a responsibility to give them a "roadmap" in advance describing where you will be taking them during the meeting. Your agenda should also include the start and end times for the meeting so that others can plan accordingly.

If you do provide an agenda for your meetings, it is critical that you manage the meeting to the agenda. Do not allow others to "hijack" the meeting to achieve other purposes. You are in control, so you have every right to tell others to schedule a separate meeting for their issues. Managing to the agenda also means finishing the meeting at or before the scheduled end time.

Please refer to the Takeaway Tool in Appendix B for a sample meeting agenda.

Score: 2	Coaches' Recommendations

You feel you can do better in this area, and it is critical to your personal time management and that of others that you do. Meetings can be very productive or they can be a complete waste of time (and very expensive); it is up to you. People attending your meeting expect you to manage it well and to achieve its objectives in the stated amount of time. If other issues arise, put them in a "parking lot" to deal with in the event there is time remaining and, if not, to be put on an agenda for another meeting. Always keep a list of action items, and publish and distribute them as soon as possible after a meeting.

Please refer to the Takeaway Tool in Appendix B for a sample meeting agenda.

I manage meeting agendas appropriately.

Your Score: 1 (strongly disagree) 2 (disagree) 3 (agree) 4 (strongly agree)

Score: 3	Coaches' Recommendations

You feel you do well in this area, but there is room for improvement. Strive to make all meetings worthwhile and managed well. Most meetings need an agenda and it should be sent to attendees well before the meeting to help them plan.

You feel you manage most meetings well but we encourage you to develop your skills in this area so that every meeting is in alignment with its agenda and achieves its objectives. You also have a responsibility as a leader to ensure that meetings you attend are also well managed and beneficial. If not, provide feedback to the meeting leader after the meeting and help them improve their skills and behaviors in this area.

Please refer to the Takeaway Tool in Appendix B for a sample meeting agenda.

Score: 4	Coaches' Recommendations

Congratulations on the excellent score for this important item. Continue to model this behavior and further develop your meeting management skills. As a leader it is important to the organization that you help others improve their skills in development meeting agendas and managing meetings.

Consider developing a meeting management norm for your organization by stating what meetings should look like, how they should be managed and what is required of those leading the meeting and those who are participating. You should work hard to ensure that every meeting in your organization is valuable and achieves its objectives.

Please refer to the Takeaway Tool in Appendix C for a sample Norm Statement for meeting management in an organization.

I manage meeting agendas appropriately.

List the development steps you will take to improve in this item.

1.

2.

3.

4.

Other Notes:

I make the best use of my time.

Isn't it nice at the end of the day to say to yourself, "That was a productive day and I used all my time wisely!" Unfortunately, many people get to the end of the day and think back on all the distractions they allowed or the time they wasted doing things that were not important or not high on their priority list.

Coaches' Challenge

How do you feel at the end of the day? Do you usually feel that you spent your time wisely? Or, do you feel you wasted a lot of time? Which is more prevalent? You may not ever get it perfect, but if you get through most days feeling you made the best use of your time you are on the right track. Do you spend your time more unwisely than wisely?

On the next two pages, circle the score you gave yourself for this statement in the "Know Your Heading" exercise. Then, read the Coaches' Recommendations for your score.

"Take care of the minutes and the hours will take care of themselves."
- Lord Chesterfield

I make the best use of my time.

Your Score: 1 (strongly disagree) 2 (disagree) 3 (agree) 4 (strongly agree)

Score: 1	Coaches' Recommendations

This was a tough item to be honest with and we appreciate your candor. We first recommend that you begin to change your behaviors immediately. If you feel you normally do not make the best use of your time it can be very depressive on your spirit.

How are you wasting your time? We also recommend that you meet with a trusted colleague (peer) and ask them to be your accountability partner. Have them monitor your time and point out to you where you waste time. We recommend that you do this with a peer who does well with time management and is sincerely interested in your success.

If you do not use an accountability partner, be accountable to yourself. Track your time doing things that are not productive. Examine how much time you waste each day and week. Next, put some rules in place that will guide your behaviors. For example, a rule could be that you do not check anything on Facebook when at work. Another rule could be that you will organize your office each Friday afternoon to help you be more productive the following week. Put the list of rules on a 3x5 card and carry it with you.

Score: 2	Coaches' Recommendations

You perceive that you do not manage your time well and waste too much. We recommend that you list the time wasters and make a set of rules to follow that will eliminate them. Most time wasters are self-directed, although some may be due to your organization's rules and policies. Focus on behaviors that you can change. List them and resolve not to engage in activities that waste your time. Remember, you only have a limited amount of time and it is your responsibility to use it wisely. You should identify the true time wasters – those minutes that have no benefit to you.

Please refer to Takeaway Tool in Appendix A to help determine your time wasters.

I make the best use of my time.

Your Score: 1 (strongly disagree) 2 (disagree) 3 (agree) 4 (strongly agree)

Score: 3	Coaches' Recommendations

This is a good score for this item, but you probably feel you do waste some time and want to improve. It should be easy for you to identify your time wasters. Once you do, think about how you can eliminate some of these behaviors. For example, if you spent too much time in "water cooler" talk, think about how you can eliminate much of the wasted time – perhaps you bring your own water and therefore do not need to leave your workspace.

As a leader you set the example in this area, and you do well. However, you also have a responsibility to show others you are keeping busy and being productive. If you have ways that you save time, share them with others on your team. Also as a leader, if you see any of your direct reports regularly wasting time, bring it to their attention and help them change their behaviors.

Score: 4	Coaches' Recommendations

Congratulations for the excellent score for this item. Leaders must set the example in this area and if a leader wastes time, followers will do so as well. Great leaders are focused and very concerned that every minute counts. If you have peers who do not do well in this area, don't hesitate to give them feedback and coach them on how to improve. If any of your direct reports regularly wastes time, bring it to their attention and work with them to improve.

I make the best use of my time.

List the development steps you will take to improve in this item.

1.

2.

3.

4.

Other Notes:

I make the best use of others' time.

We often don't think about how we are using others' time – it is their responsibility. But an effective leader is constantly aware of how they are using others' time. Leaders must ensure that they area respectful of others' time and they are conscious of how much time they use when engaging others. Leaders not only have the responsibility of not wasting others' time, they have a responsibility to make the best use of others' time by ensuring that the tasks they assign are appropriate for their individual skill level.

Coaches' Challenge

Have you ever thought, "I wish Joe would stay away from me, he is a total waste of my time. He doesn't talk about anything serious and I don't enjoy his talking about sports all the time." Others are usually not aware they are consuming our time when they talk with us and don't think of being respectful of our time. What about you? Are you respectful of others' time?

On the next two pages, circle the score you gave yourself for this statement in the "Know Your Heading" exercise. Then, read the Coaches' Recommendations for your score.

"One thing you can't recycle is wasted time."

- Unknown

I make the best use of others' time.

Your Score: 1 (strongly disagree) 2 (disagree) 3 (agree) 4 (strongly agree)

Score: 1	Coaches' Recommendations

Your first step is to identify how you are wasting others' time. Do you engage them in idle chit-chat when they are busy or responsible for getting something done? Or, do you not make the best use of their time because you assign them tasks that are not appropriate for their skill level? Perhaps you assign easy tasks to someone who has a high skill level and becomes bored easily. On the other hand, you could also assign tasks to someone who will struggle with the tasks because they do not have the skill set required.

As a leader you must be concerned about your influence on others' time, a valuable commodity to them. Before engaging in a discussion with someone, think about what you want to say and whether you should say it to this person. Think about tasks that you need to assign and be sure to engage the right person who will be challenged but at the same time competent to do the tasks.

Score: 2	Coaches' Recommendations

It is important that you monitor your behaviors to improve in this area. People don't like having their time wasted. It is one thing if they fall into bad habits and waste their own time; it is another if their time is wasted by a leader. Leaders should set the example in this area and consciously think about the impact they have on others' time.

Beginning today, refrain from idle talk with others unless it is an appropriate time and place. Before assigning tasks, make sure you are engaging the right person who will be challenged but have the skill set to achieve success. Be careful to not assign tasks to people who do not have the skills to achieve success with a task or project.

Remember, if you are wasting another's time you are probably wasting your own time as well.

I make the best use of others' time.

Your Score: 1 (strongly disagree) 2 (disagree) 3 (agree) 4 (strongly agree)

Score: 3	Coaches' Recommendations

Good score for this item, but we suspect you also can think of times when you have not made the best use of others' time. As a leader you need to consider who the best person is for a task and assign accordingly. You want someone to be challenged but also be in a position they can succeed without using an excessive amount of time.

Leaders must also set the example by not wasting others' time in extended idle talk or meaningless discussions. Some of this is tolerable since leaders also want to get to know people and build relationships. However, it is important that these types of conversations be kept to a minimum and be of short duration when they occur during normal work time.

Score: 4	Coaches' Recommendations

This is an excellent score for this item. You clearly set the example in this area and are not perceived as someone who wastes others' time. This not only gives you a good reputation, but also enhances your credibility.

Consider your colleagues. Are there fellow leaders who are noted for wasting the time of others or not making the best use of others' time by assigning them tasks that are beneath their skill level or beyond their skill level? If so, you have an opportunity to give them feedback and coach them to take steps to improve in this important area.

I make the best use of others' time.

List the development steps you will take to improve in this item.

1.

2.

3.

4.

Other Notes:

I manage meetings according to the communicated schedule.

No one likes meetings that start late or go past the scheduled end time. Others have schedules to meet and work to do. It is incumbent upon the leader of the meeting to always start on time and end either before the scheduled time or right at the scheduled time. There are no excuses in this area. If a leader calls a meeting and determines the amount of time it will take to achieve the objectives, sets the start time and end time, it is their responsibility to adhere to the schedule and the agenda.

Coaches' Challenge

How many times have you been in a meeting and the leader says, "So and so is not here yet, we will wait a few minutes for her to arrive." How did that make you feel as time dragged on? What if a meeting was to be over at a specific time and you had another important event or meeting scheduled right after it – and the meeting goes into overtime? How do you react? Have you ever told a meeting leader, "I will be a few minutes late, please wait for me?"

On the next two pages, circle the score you gave yourself for this statement in the "Know Your Heading" exercise. Then, read the Coaches' Recommendations for your score.

"He who knows most, grieves most for wasted time."
- Dante

I manage meetings according to the communicated schedule.

Your Score: 1 (strongly disagree) 2 (disagree) 3 (agree) 4 (strongly agree)

Score: 1	Coaches' Recommendations

You must change your behavior immediately. If you call a meeting for a specific time and you invite people, begin at the established time, regardless if everyone is present or not. You are the leader of the meeting and there is no excuse for not beginning on time. If a key person is not present, consider how you would begin by covering agenda topics that are less relevant to the key person. If you cannot do this, begin anyway. If the person shows up late, be polite and provide a summary of what has been discussed or decided so far.

It is also critical that your meeting ends on time (or before). People may very well have other meetings, events or tasks planned and must leave your meeting on time. Don't try to fill up the meeting time with idle chat – just because you scheduled an hour doesn't mean you have to use the entire hour. If you accomplish your objectives, end the meeting. People will be grateful for the time you have given them.

Score: 2	Coaches' Recommendations

You feel you need to improve in this area and we highly recommend that you change your behaviors in managing meeting times. If you call a meeting for a specific time and you invite people, begin at the established time, regardless if everyone is present or not. You are the leader of the meeting and there is no excuse for not beginning on time. If a key person is not present, consider how you would begin by covering agenda topics that are less relevant to the key person. If you cannot do this, begin anyway.
It is also critical that your meeting ends on time (or before). People may very well have other meetings, events or tasks planned and must leave your meeting on time. Don't try to fill up the meeting time with idle chat – just because you scheduled an hour doesn't mean you have to use the entire hour. If you accomplish your objectives, end the meeting. People will be grateful for the time you have given them.

I manage meetings according to the communicated schedule.

Your Score: 1 (strongly disagree) 2 (disagree) 3 (agree) 4 (strongly agree)

Score: 3	Coaches' Recommendations

You gave yourself a good score for this item. We suspect, however, that you can identify instances where you did not begin a meeting on time or end a meeting as scheduled. If that is the case, how did people react? As you know, people's time is very important. You need to continue to be respectful of others' time and be 100% in compliance for this item. Continue to manage meetings according to the communicated schedule.

Consider setting meeting Norms for your organization. See the Takeaway Tool in Appendix C for an example of meeting Norms.

Score: 4	Coaches' Recommendations

Excellent score for this item. Continue to model this behavior. As a leader it is your responsibility to ensure that others manage meetings according to the schedule as well. If you are waiting for a meeting to begin and it is being managed by a peer or a direct report, don't hesitate to tell them to begin at the appointed time. Also, if you see the meeting end time is approaching and there are still agenda items to consider, be an advocate for setting a second meeting to continue the discussion. Don't let the meeting go beyond its scheduled end time. Be assertive and others will begin to model your behaviors.

Consider setting meeting Norms for your organization. See the Takeaway Tool in Appendix C for an example of meeting Norms.

I manage meetings according to the communicated schedule.

List the development steps you will take to improve in this item.

1.

2.

3.

4.

Other Notes:

I meet deadlines.

Whether you meet deadlines or not is an indicator of how well you use time management skills and behaviors. If you consistently miss deadlines, you are not managing your time well. Yes, sometimes a deadline is missed for some other reasons, but if you are known for missing many deadlines, look at how you manage your time. Deadlines are a part of most jobs and failing to meet them can have a very negative effect on your career. Usually, we know the deadline far enough in advance to meet it, but because of procrastination and failure to establish priorities correctly, deadlines are often missed.

> ### *Coaches' Challenge*
>
> *Deadlines can make time management easier. If a deadline is set, simply figure out how to get it done in the allotted time, along with everything else you have to do. How do you feel about deadlines? What if you gave a deadline to tasks that do not have a deadline assigned? Would that help you?*

On the next two pages, circle the score you gave yourself for this statement in the "Know Your Heading" exercise. Then, read the Coaches' Recommendations for your score.

"What may be done at any time will be done at no time."
- Scottish Proverb

I meet deadlines.

Your Score: 1 (strongly disagree) 2 (disagree) 3 (agree) 4 (strongly agree)

Score: 1	Coaches' Recommendations

Not meeting deadlines can be a career stopper so the time to correct this is now. Vow to make every deadline moving forward and to do it with quality. Assess why you are missing most of your deadlines. If it is a time management problem, how can you change your behaviors? We recommend that you keep a running list of all deadlines describing what needs to be done, the deadline and who is the stakeholder. Review this list every day and integrate it into your "to-do" list and ensure that the items have the correct priority.

You should also estimate how much time it will take for each task with a deadline. If something is going to take 3 days to accomplish, you can't start it the day before it is due. Planning is essential. We recommend you create your deadline list, establish priorities, and integrate into your daily schedule; giving yourself sufficient time to complete all tasks.

Score: 2	Coaches' Recommendations

You see the need to improve in this area and we recommend that you focus your time management improvement in this area. Deadlines are important. If you become known for missing many of them it can have a negative effect on your career. Keep a list of all tasks with a deadline. Estimate how long it will take to complete each task and then give yourself a start date to begin work on the task with sufficient time to complete it before it is due.

Review your deadline list daily and ensure that each task has the correct priority and sufficient time to complete it with quality before the deadline. Integrate your deadline list into your daily "to-do" list and focus on getting things done ahead of schedule instead of being late every time.

I meet deadlines.

Your Score: 1 (strongly disagree) 2 (disagree) 3 (agree) 4 (strongly agree)

Score: 3	Coaches' Recommendations

This is a good score for this item. Continue to meet your deadlines with quality. Review your task list and deadlines frequently and ensure that you have the right priorities for your work and also that you have sufficient time to complete each task before it is due. As a leader, you set the example in this area. You can't expect others to meet their deadlines if you do not. Be consistent.

Talk to your team members to stress the importance of deadlines. If you have anyone who is having a problem meeting deadlines, talk with them and encourage them to manage their time better so that they can be consistent in meeting deadlines.

Score: 4	Coaches' Recommendations

This is an excellent score for this item and we recommend that you continue to meet your deadlines; as a leader you set the example to others. Your role should be to help others understand the importance of deadlines and remove any obstacles they have to fulfilling their responsibilities in this area.

If you have peers or direct reports who have difficulties achieving their deadlines, work with them to understand why they are having a problem. Perhaps they are having a problem assigning the priority to each task, or they may not be putting in the time or effort needed to get their work done on time. Your responsibility is to help them realize the root of their problem and to encourage them to take action to improve.

Part 3 – Development Recommendations

I meet deadlines.

List the development steps you will take to improve in this item.

1.

2.

3.

4.

Other Notes:

I prioritize my tasks to insure important responsibilities are fulfilled.

It is one thing to list all the tasks you are required to do, it is another to know which are the most important to complete. Prioritization is a key step in planning what you need to be working on. Leaders must not only prioritize their own tasks but also help their peers and direct reports understand what is most important.

Coaches' Challenge

How do you prioritize your tasks? Many people use an A, B, C system where A is the highest priority and the most urgent tasks and C are those tasks that are the lowest priority and not the most urgent. Review your "to-do" list and assign priorities according to the A, B, C system.

On the next two pages, circle the score you gave yourself for this statement in the "Know Your Heading" exercise. Then, read the Coaches' Recommendations for your score.

"It is your responsibility to know what is important and do what is important. focusing on the unimportant will make you unimportant."
- Galen Schmit

I prioritize my tasks to insure important responsibilities are fulfilled.

Your Score: 1 (strongly disagree)   2 (disagree)   3 (agree)   4 (strongly agree)

Score: 1	Coaches' Recommendations

You clearly need a system for prioritizing your tasks that works for you. Please read the section on prioritization on page 44. Think about what works for you. If you are having difficulty determining the priority of a task, talk to the person who assigned the task to you. Remember, they may think their task is the highest priority, but compared to the other tasks on your list it may not be your highest priority. You need to seek out information from others to make the determination of the priority of each task on your list. If you are still having difficulty, talk with your leader or manager. How do they assess the priority of each task?

Often, high priority tasks are the most difficult for us, so we procrastinate and do not get them done by the deadline. Make it a point to work according to the priorities you have set, regardless of the difficulty of the task.

Score: 2	Coaches' Recommendations

You feel you could improve in this area. Your first step should be to identify a system for prioritizing that works for you. Please see the section on prioritization on page 44. Determine what system would work best for you and adopt it moving forward. If you have difficulty determining the priority of a specific task, talk to the person who assigned it to you to learn more about its importance. If you are still unsure, talk with your leader or manager to get help determining what you should be working on.

Often, high priority tasks are the most difficult for us, so we procrastinate and do not get them done by the deadline. Make it a point to work according to the priorities you have set, regardless of the difficulty of the task.

I prioritize my tasks to insure important responsibilities are fulfilled.

Your Score: 1 (strongly disagree) 2 (disagree) 3 (agree) 4 (strongly agree)

Score: 3	Coaches' Recommendations

You feel you do well in this area, but there may be room for improvement. Are you sometimes unclear about what the priority of a task should be? If so, talk with the person who assigned the task or your leader or manager. Sometimes it helps to hear another perspective on how a task should be prioritized.

We strongly recommend that you use a system to prioritize your tasks. Please see the section on prioritization on page 44. Try the different systems and adopt whichever one is best for you.

Score: 4	Coaches' Recommendations

This is an excellent score and we are pleased that you do well prioritizing your tasks. Your role as a leader is to also help others who may be having difficulty in this area. Be sure to give clear instructions when assigning tasks and let people know what you expect of them. If they have other tasks to accomplish, review their list and give them your feedback on what their priority should be. If they have tasks assigned from other leaders, don't be presumptuous and tell them your tasks are most important. Be objective and help them determine the right priority.

If you have a conflict with another leader regarding the priority of a task someone should be doing, talk with your colleague and learn more about their expectations. Negotiate with them regarding what should be done first and then communicate the results to the person who is assigned to complete the task.

I prioritize my tasks to insure important responsibilities are fulfilled.

List the development steps you will take to improve in this item.

1.

2.

3.

4.

Other Notes:

I respond in a timely manner to requests.

We are bombarded every day with requests from others. Each person requesting something of us feels they are our highest priority. When we don't respond because we have other (higher) priorities, people get upset and claim that we don't care about their needs. There are simple solutions to this dilemma, but your first step is to respond as quickly as possible whenever you can.

> ### *Coaches' Challenge*
>
> *Think about the demands you put on other people. Sometimes leaders don't realize it when they are overburdening other people. Are your requests legitimate? Are they fully explained? If something can wait, do you communicate that to the person you are tasking?*

On the next two pages, circle the score you gave yourself for this statement in the "Know Your Heading" exercise. Then, read the Coaches' Recommendations for your score.

"You cannot do a kindness too soon,
for you never know how soon it will be too late."
- Ralph Waldo Emerson

I respond in a timely manner to requests.

Your Score: 1 (strongly disagree) 2 (disagree) 3 (agree) 4 (strongly agree)

Score: 1	Coaches' Recommendations

Why are you not responsive to others' requests? Your first step is to seriously think about why you do not respond in a timely manner. Is it because you have too much to do? Are you responsive to some people's requests but not to others? If so, why? How do you react to a person who makes a request that you know you cannot fulfill in a timely manner? Communication is key – if you cannot respond to someone's request immediately, you have a responsibility to tell them and to negotiate a clear expectation on when you can respond.

You are expected to be responsive. However, your timeframe for responding is dependent on many factors, including who is making the request. When you are asked to do something, assess when you can have it done and provide this information to the requester. Without communication around expectations, assumptions will be made and expectations will not be met.

Score: 2	Coaches' Recommendations

This is an area in which you think you need improvement. Assess why you are not always responsive to others' requests. Is it a communication issue? When negotiating requests for your efforts or time, always be clear on what you can and cannot do. Ask for help in prioritizing if that is the issue. If you simply have too much to do to respond to the person's request, be honest and tell them immediately about your situation. If they feel their request is still a priority, work with them to negotiate with others who are putting demands on you.

Communication is the key to understanding so you can do what is expected of you by others.

I respond in a timely manner to requests.

Your Score: 1 (strongly disagree)   2 (disagree)   3 (agree)   4 (strongly agree)

Score: 3	Coaches' Recommendations

This is a very good score for this item and we recommend that you continue to be responsive to others' requests. It is not always easy but you seem to be successful in this area. Always be clear on expectations about something assigned to you or a request being made of your skills or time.

If you cannot respond to someone's request in a timely manner, be transparent and tell the person up front. Do not wait until you miss the deadline and do not meet their expectations. Do your best to be responsive, but at the same time, be clear about what you can and cannot do for others. Learn how to say "No."

Score: 4	Coaches' Recommendations

This is an excellent score for this item and we congratulate you for your responsiveness. Continue to model this behavior. Think about your requests to others. Are you clear on your expectations? Do you request too much of one specific person because you trust them more than others? How could you be more equitable in your requests?

Always be clear on your expectations of others. Encourage an environment where people are comfortable challenging you, and telling you they cannot meet your expectations and want to discuss further if that is the case. People want to be responsive but sometimes feel they cannot communicate their reality to others because it may look like failure.

I respond in a timely manner to requests.

List the development steps you will take to improve in this item.

1.

2.

3.

4.

Other Notes:

I use time management techniques and tools to streamline efficiency and productivity.

Time management tools can be a great help to anyone with a busy schedule and many tasks to accomplish. But, by the same token, people can become "slaves" to their technology and waste valuable time maintaining all the devices and applications they are trying to use to increase productivity. We recommend a balance whereby you choose what tools you are going to use; learn to use them well and stick with them. This minimizes the time spent constantly learning a new system and updating.

Coaches' Challenge

What time management tools do you use? Are you "up to date" and using a technology-based tool or do you still use a "to-do" list on paper? Are you happy with how you use your time management tools? What improvements would you like to see?

On the next two pages, circle the score you gave yourself for this statement in the "Know Your Heading" exercise. Then, read the Coaches' Recommendations for your score.

"Time is on my side."

\- Mick Jagger

I use time management techniques and tools to streamline efficiency and productivity.

Your Score: 1 (strongly disagree) 2 (disagree) 3 (agree) 4 (strongly agree)

Score: 1	Coaches' Recommendations

It is important that every leader use tools to manage their time. This can be as simple as a paper-written "to-do" list updated every day. If you are not using any tools to manage your time, please review our comments on time management tools, beginning on page 76. Think of the effects of not using any time management tools. Do you forget meetings? Do you have difficulty remembering everything you need to do? Do you have problems prioritizing tasks? Take the time to investigate time management tools and select a couple to try out. If you are minimally technologically oriented, try to use a tool that is computer based. If you have an iPhone or iPad, check the applications that are available.

Regardless what tool you choose to manage your time, stick with it for a month so that you can see results. If you find the tool cumbersome after a month, change to a simpler one that meets your needs.

Score: 2	Coaches' Recommendations

You feel you could improve in this area. Please review our comments on time management tools, beginning on page 76. Are you unhappy with how you use tools to manage your time and tasks? If so, consider the alternatives that are available. If you use an iPhone or iPad, there are many applications that can be downloaded to help manage your time.

It is important that you use a time management tool that you are comfortable with and meets your needs. Ask others what systems they use and why they are comfortable with each. Find the best tool for you and stick with it for a month. If it doesn't work for you, consider another tool and give it a try.

There are tools that can help you manage your time and tasks. It benefits you to find the tool that works best for you and use it to your advantage.

I use time management techniques and tools to streamline efficiency and productivity.

Your Score: 1 (strongly disagree) 2 (disagree) 3 (agree) 4 (strongly agree)

Score: 3	Coaches' Recommendations

This is a good score for this item and you appear to be comfortable with the time management tools that you use. Consider, however, that there may be other tools now on the market that would be of even greater benefit. For example, if you are using Microsoft Outlook to manage your time and tasks, and you have an iPhone or iPad, do you synchronize them to have your task list and calendar available on your mobile device?

You may be doing well with your current tools, but there may also be additional ways you can use your favorite tool to help you become even more productive.

Score: 4	Coaches' Recommendations

This is an excellent score for this item and you are happy with how you use time management tools to manage your time and tasks. Consider your peers and direct reports. Do they use time management tools effectively? If not, how can you convince them of the benefits of using the same system as you? Is there an enterprise-wide system that could be used in your organization, such as shared calendars?

As a leader you want to not only model the use of time management tools, but also help the organization communicate better and be more in alignment by using common tools and systems.

I use time management techniques and tools to streamline efficiency and productivity.

List the development steps you will take to improve in this item.

1.

2.

3.

4.

Other Notes:

I always arrive at meetings or events on time.

Time is money and it is amazing sometimes how we forget that. If a meeting is delayed it can be very expensive. In addition, being late for a meeting or an event is simply disrespectful. Yes, there are times when it is unavoidable, but most times people are late because they are not good at time management and are busy doing something else.

Coaches' Challenge

Here's a math problem: There is a meeting scheduled at 2:00 for 12 managers. The meeting is delayed 15 minutes due to 3 key managers being late. If the managers make an average of $150 per hour (including benefits), what does the delay cost? The answer is $450! This is the cost before the meeting even began.

On the next two pages, circle the score you gave yourself for this statement in the "Know Your Heading" exercise. Then, read the Coaches' Recommendations for your score.

"The key is not spending time, but in investing it."
- Stephen R. Covey

I always arrive at meetings or events on time.

Your Score: 1 (strongly disagree) 2 (disagree) 3 (agree) 4 (strongly agree)

Score: 1	Coaches' Recommendations

Your behavior in this area should change immediately. If you are consistently late for meetings or other events, you are being disrespectful of others' time. If you are late because you are busy doing something else, make it a habit to drop what you are doing to be at the meeting – and schedule designated time before the meeting to prepare. It is disrespectful if you are late for a meeting and also unprepared.

Does this happen when you call a meeting or are the person assigned to manage the meeting? If so, it is even more critical that you take steps to be prepared and be on time.

Score: 2	Coaches' Recommendations

You need improvement in this area. If you are consistently late for meetings or events, you are being disrespectful of others' time. If you are late because you are busy doing something else, make it a habit to drop what you are doing to be at the meeting – and schedule designated time before the meeting to prepare. It is disrespectful if you are late for a meeting and also unprepared.

Does this happen when you call a meeting or are the person assigned to manage the meeting? If so, it is even more critical that you take steps to be prepared and be on time.

I always arrive at meetings or events on time.

Your Score: 1 (strongly disagree)   2 (disagree)   3 (agree)   4 (strongly agree)

Score: 3	Coaches' Recommendations

This is a good score for this item; however, you feel there is room for improvement. If you know you are going to be late for a meeting or event, notify someone so that the event will not be held up waiting for you. If you are late because of another meeting going overtime, consider leaving the previous meeting with the justification that you have another meeting – perhaps the initial meeting could have been managed better to avoid the overrun.

As a leader you are expected to set the example in this area. If you are late others will notice and assume that the behavior is OK and they can be late in the future.

Score: 4	Coaches' Recommendations

This is an excellent score and we encourage you to continue to model this behavior. As a leader, however, it is also important that you address your concerns to others who may be consistently late for meetings or events. If any of your direct reports have this issue, don't hesitate to give them feedback and reiterate your expectations. If a team member has this problem and it is due to time management difficulties, we encourage you to give them a copy of this workbook to focus on their improvement.

If a peer leader is consistently late, you also have the responsibility to discuss the effects of their behavior with them.

I always arrive at meetings or events on time.

List the development steps you will take to improve in this item.

1.

2.

3.

4.

Other Notes:

I do tasks according to their criticality and importance and do not procrastinate.

Procrastinate means to put off or delay. Often, people procrastinate on difficult or uninteresting tasks. They think it is much more productive to focus on easy or exciting tasks. Meanwhile, the delayed tasks do not get completed. Effective leaders work on a priority system where the most critical and important tasks are the ones that get attention first.

Coaches' Challenge

Did you ever think how much stress procrastination adds to you? You know a task is critical and needs to be done, but you procrastinate. This serves to add considerable stress to you and possibly others. Doesn't it feel better when we complete an important or critical task on time, without any delays due to procrastination?

On the next two pages, circle the score you gave yourself for this statement in the "Know Your Heading" exercise. Then, read the Coaches' Recommendations for your score.

"Never leave 'till tomorrow which you can do today."
- Benjamin Franklin

I do tasks according to their criticality and importance and do not procrastinate.

Your Score: 1 (strongly disagree) 2 (disagree) 3 (agree) 4 (strongly agree)

Score: 1	Coaches' Recommendations

Procrastination is a problem that you need to face immediately and take steps to change your behavior in this area. Procrastination can be serious and prevent you from getting things done that need to be done, as you focus on getting things done that do not need to be done.

We recommend that you develop a prioritization system for all your tasks. Label each task according to its criticality and importance either A (most important), B (somewhat important) or C (not important). Then, only work on the A tasks. Do not allow yourself to be drawn into "knocking off" easy tasks. Consider having an "accountability partner." This person would review your priorities with you each morning and determine how successful you have been in the previous day in focusing on high-priority tasks.

Score: 2	Coaches' Recommendations

You feel you can improve in this area and apparently you procrastinate enough that it makes you uncomfortable and less productive. Your first step should be to label the priority of each task – A for most important and most critical, B for those that are somewhat important, and C for those that are not important. Once you have categorized your tasks according to their criticality and importance, only work on the A tasks until they are completed. Then, you can focus on the B tasks.

Your priority list should be a living list that you review each morning, at a minimum. Some tasks that are a B can become A tasks, and so on. Reviewing and modifying your priorities is important and a key factor for leadership success.

You may also consider having an accountability partner to review your priorities on a regular basis to ensure that you are correct in how you are categorizing them.

I do tasks according to their criticality and importance and do not procrastinate.

Your Score: 1 (strongly disagree)   2 (disagree)   3 (agree)   4 (strongly agree)

Score: 3	Coaches' Recommendations

This is a good score for this important item. Since you normally do not procrastinate, be on the lookout for times that you may do it and not realize it. Excuses for not working on something difficult can come easy. You should always ask yourself, "Is this the most important and critical task that I need to be working on at the moment?" If not, refocus your efforts toward those tasks that are most important.

There are times, however, when we do not have the time or inclination to do the most difficult tasks – it may not be our "peak performance time of the day." In that case, it is OK to do some less important tasks, if you schedule the important task to be done at a better time. This should be rare, however. Begin each day with a review of the most important and critical tasks that need to be accomplished. Set your goals for the day based on this review.

Score: 4	Coaches' Recommendations

This is an excellent score for this item and it benefits you greatly to not procrastinate. As a leader, however, you must monitor your direct reports and peers. If you see any of them developing bad habits in this area, you should provide them with feedback and assistance in this area. Some people may not be aware that they are procrastinating. Feedback from you may be just what they need.

Your direct reports may need help prioritizing their tasks. They may feel that every task you assign to them is important and critical. You need to give them an indication of your expectations and how critical each task is in comparison with their other assignments.

I do tasks according to their criticality and importance and do not procrastinate.

List the development steps you will take to improve in this item.

1.

2.

3.

4.

Other Notes:

I know how much time I am spending on various jobs I do.

A lot of people have no idea how they spend their time. It is important for many reasons why you should be concerned about how you spend your time. Knowing how long a task takes is important information when allocating time in the future. Tracking your time also enables you to see where you are wasting time. It doesn't have to be difficult or cumbersome to keep track of your time; there are many programs and applications that can help. But, we have found that the best system is a plain notebook that lists how you spend your time can be the easiest way to know how much time you are spending on each task.

Coaches' Challenge

How many times, at the end of the day, have you said, "Where did the day go?" or, "I don't feel like I got anything done today." If that happens to you, consider tracking your time to see what you are really working on. Most importantly, track the amount of time you are giving to non-work things – breaks, idle conversations, Facebook, LinkedIn, etc. It may be quite revealing!

On the next two pages, circle the score you gave yourself for this statement in the "Know Your Heading" exercise. Then, read the Coaches' Recommendations for your score.

"In truth, people can generally make time for what they choose to do; it is not really the time but the will that is lacking."

- Sir John Lubbock

124

I know how much time I am spending on various jobs I do.

Your Score: 1 (strongly disagree)   2 (disagree)   3 (agree)   4 (strongly agree)

Score: 1	Coaches' Recommendations

Beginning today you need to adopt a system to track your time. The fact that you don't know how you are spending your time is typically an admission that you are not making the best use of your time. Commit to using a program or application that tracks your time or, to keep it simple, use a small notebook that lists your tasks (and categories of time wasters) and monitor your time. Do this for a week, at a minimum. At the end of that week, analyze how you spent your time. What changes would you make to improve your productivity? How much time did you spend "goofing off?" How much time did you spend on tasks that should have been delayed because they were not high priority?

Identify three changes you will make during the following week to improve your productivity. List these changes on a 3x5 card and keep it with you to review periodically.

Score: 2	Coaches' Recommendations

It is important to know how you spend your time. One reason is that keeping track of your time for a period will help you see where you are wasting time. If you track your time honestly you will be able to identify habits that you want to change to be more productive. Another reason for tracking your time is to improve your planning. If you have done a task before you can use that data to plan your schedule when you are faced with doing the same task again. A third reason for tracking your time is that just by doing so you increase your awareness of what you are doing and you will tend to avoid unproductive activities.

Beginning today, use a method to track your time for one week. At the end of the week, analyze the results and identify three ways you will improve the following week. Do this each week until you see noticeable improvement in your time management.

I know how much time I am spending on various jobs I do.

Your Score: 1 (strongly disagree) 2 (disagree) 3 (agree) 4 (strongly agree)

Score: 3	Coaches' Recommendations

This is a good score for this item and we encourage you to continue to track your time on various tasks. Think about how you could improve further. Are there tasks you are doing that are not productive? How much time do you spend in meetings that are not productive? How much time do you spend in idle conversation?

As a leader it is important that you manage your time well. Knowing how much time you spend on various tasks helps you to plan better and be more productive. You also need to know how much time your team is spending on tasks. Carefully explain the importance of time tracking to your team and get their agreement without their feeling as though they are being micro-managed.

Score: 4	Coaches' Recommendations

This is an excellent score and we urge you to continue to be aware of how you spend your time. Just as important, as a leader you need to know how much time your team is spending on various tasks. This helps you plan better for future projects. It is difficult, however, to get your team members to track their time. Leaders must explain the importance of knowing how much time is spent on a task without making team members feel they are being micro-managed. Be careful in how you position your need to know what team members are doing.

By the same token, you may have team members who are not productive and do not make the best use of their time. If so, don't hesitate to coach them and give them tools, such as tracking their time, to enable them to succeed at improving their habits.

I know how much time I am spending on various jobs I do.

List the development steps you will take to improve in this item.

1.

2.

3.

4.

Other Notes:

I am organized and it is easy for me to find what I need.

Organized people are much more productive than those who "look busy but can't find their own two feet." How does organization relate to time management? Think about how long it takes to find something that you need. This is all wasted time. Think about how many times you needed something and could never find it. Being organized is a tool to help you manage your time better.

> ### *Coaches' Challenge*
>
> *Look around your work area. Is it tidy and is everything in its place? Look at your computer desktop. Is it well organized? Can you find files easily – both paper and electronic? Is your calendar up to date? Do you maintain a task list? What are your goals for the day?*

On the next two pages, circle the score you gave yourself for this statement in the "Know Your Heading" exercise. Then, read the Coaches' Recommendations for your score.

"The surest way to be late is to have plenty of time."
- Leo Kennedy

I am organized and it is easy for me to find what I need.

Your Score: 1 (strongly disagree) 2 (disagree) 3 (agree) 4 (strongly agree)

Score: 1	Coaches' Recommendations

It is good that you realize you are not organized. Now is the time to do something about it. First, organize your workspace – today is a great day to get started. If it is very bad – get help from an assistant or someone you know who is very good at organization. Your workspace needs to be organized so that you do not waste time hunting for what you need. Everything has its place and if you keep it in its place you will know where to find it when you need it.

Next, get your phone numbers, addresses and other needed information in order. Update your contact lists. You should also keep a daily "to-do" list to help keep track of what you need to be focusing on. Look at your computer "desktop." Do your electronic files need to be organized as well?

At the end of each day take the time to clean your desk and put away anything you will not need the next morning. Being organized is simply developing new habits.

Score: 2	Coaches' Recommendations

First, organize your workspace – today is a great day to get started. Your workspace needs to be organized so you do not waste time hunting for what you need. Everything has its place and if you keep it in its place you will know where to find it when needed.

Next, get your phone numbers, addresses and other needed information in order. Update your contact lists. You should also keep a daily "to-do" list to help you keep track of what you need to be focusing on. Look at your computer "desktop." Do your electronic files need to be organized as well? At the end of each day take the time to clean your desk and put away anything you will not need the next morning. Being organized is simply developing new habits.

I am organized and it is easy for me to find what I need.

Your Score: 1 (strongly disagree) 2 (disagree) 3 (agree) 4 (strongly agree)

Score: 3	Coaches' Recommendations

This is a good score for this item but we sense that you realize you could be a bit more organized. Assess where you could improve – your office? Your computer files? Your "to-do" list? Your contact list? Decide where you want to focus and make the time to get better organized in your weakest area. Could you reorganize your office or workspace to be more efficient? Do you have a lot of files (paper and electronic) that could be thrown away or deleted? Take a few minutes each week to keep things in order.

Score: 4	Coaches' Recommendations

This is an excellent score and you most likely model organization to the rest of your team. Do you have anyone on your team who is failing in this area? If so, what would be the best way to coach them to improve their organization skills? Explain to them that they lose valuable time when they cannot find what they need quickly. Encourage them to spend time each week organizing their workspace and computer files. If you ask them for a document and they cannot quickly find it, use this as a "teaching moment" to demonstrate that they are not only wasting their time but yours as well.

I am organized and it is easy for me to find what I need.

List the development steps you will take to improve in this item.

1.

2.

3.

4.

Other Notes:

I manage interruptions well and keep them to a minimum.

We love to interrupt people, not by design or serious intent, but because we are social and love to interact with others. On the other hand, when we are concentrating on a project or task it infuriates us to be interrupted. You cannot manage your time well and be productive if you are constantly being interrupted. Take steps today to manage your interruptions so that you can focus on what you are doing.

> ### *Coaches' Challenge*
>
> *Have you ever felt like lashing out in anger when you have been interrupted while concentrating on something? What could you have done to prevent the interruption? Did you do something, like leave your door open, to invite the interruption? What can you do to signal that you do not want to be interrupted?*

On the next two pages, circle the score you gave yourself for this statement in the "Know Your Heading" exercise. Then, read the Coaches' Recommendations for your score.

"Time is really the only capital that any human being has, and the only thing he can't afford to lose."
- Thomas Edison

I manage interruptions well and keep them to a minimum.

Your Score: 1 (strongly disagree) 2 (disagree) 3 (agree) 4 (strongly agree)

Score: 1	Coaches' Recommendations

Clearly interruptions are having a negative effect on your productivity. Beginning today, take steps to minimize interruptions. If you have a door to your office, keep it closed when you are working and put a tactfully worded sign on the door to please not interrupt you. If you do not have a door to your work area, consider using headphones to mask out noise and put a sign in your area that you need to focus and desire not to be interrupted.

If you have someone who consistently interrupts you regardless of your signals, talk with the person and explain that this is a weakness of yours that you are trying to improve and you would appreciate their help by not interrupting you.

If you are being interrupted by your phone with calls and text messages, be proactive and turn your phone off while focusing on work. Turn off e-mail alerts as well if they are a source of interruption to you.

Score: 2	Coaches' Recommendations

Beginning today, take steps to minimize interruptions. If you have a door to your office, keep it closed when you are working, and put a tactfully worded sign on the door to please not interrupt you. If you do not have a door to your work area, consider using headphones to mask out noise and put a sign in your area that you need to focus and desire not to be interrupted.

If you have someone who consistently interrupts you, regardless of your signals, talk with the person and explain that this is a weakness of yours that you are trying to improve and you would appreciate their help by not interrupting you.

Just as important, be respectful of others' time and do not interrupt others when it is clear they are working and need to focus.

I manage interruptions well and keep them to a minimum.

Your Score: 1 (strongly disagree) 2 (disagree) 3 (agree) 4 (strongly agree)

Score: 3	Coaches' Recommendations

This is a good score for this item. How could you improve? Consider setting aside dedicated quiet time where people know you are not to be interrupted. During this quiet time you should also turn off your phone and not receive calls or text messages. It is not only people who interrupt us. Intruders include electronic interrupters such as phone calls, text messages, push notifications and the like. Take your management of interruptions to the next level by barring any interruption – human or electronic – during your dedicated quiet time.

Score: 4	Coaches' Recommendations

You scored well for this item but you may need to take it a step further. As a leader you are responsible for ensuring that your team works under the best conditions. If you have a chronic interrupter on your team, you have a responsibility to talk with the person and stress the impact their behavior is having on others.

You also have a responsibility to control electronic interruptions if they are a problem in your work team. In addition, set the policy for no phones or laptops during meetings unless directly related to the topic of the meeting. Set the example in this area by being respectful of others' time and concentration while they are working.

I manage interruptions well and keep them to a minimum.

List the development steps you will take to improve in this item.

1.

2.

3.

4.

Other Notes:

I leave contingency time in my schedule to deal with "the unexpected."

Some people fill their schedule to the point they don't have any free time throughout the day. This may be necessary for some people at times, but it should not be the norm. Almost every day something will happen to necessitate a change in the schedule. If your schedule is full, what do you do? Most people will do a quick "prioritization" and cancel the least important event to handle the immediate situation. What happens to the other event? It gets moved to another day and helps fill up that day's schedule. You should include free time each day to handle events or tasks that arise.

Coaches' Challenge

How full is your schedule? What if something comes up? Is it a major deal to change your schedule? What unexpected events have wreaked havoc on your schedule in the past? How did you react?

On the next two pages, circle the score you gave yourself for this statement in the "Know Your Heading" exercise. Then, read the Coaches' Recommendations for your score.

"Time is what we want most, but what we use worst."
- William Penn

I leave contingency time in my schedule to deal with "the unexpected."

Your Score: 1 (strongly disagree) 2 (disagree) 3 (agree) 4 (strongly agree)

Score: 1	Coaches' Recommendations

Clearly, things that happen outside your normal schedule are disruptive to you. Moving forward, we recommend that you build time into your schedule to handle things that are unexpected. Try to schedule at least an hour in the morning and an hour later in the day to be able to react to unexpected meetings and tasks. This gives you the flexibility to move things around if necessary.

What if nothing unexpected happens during a day? Count the scheduled open time as time you can be working on other longer-term tasks, getting organized, or reaching out to customers or direct reports to build relationships. Look on the open time as a gift when it is not needed. You should have no trouble using the open time when it is not needed for something unexpected.

Score: 2	Coaches' Recommendations

Stuff happens! Effective leaders are able to adapt to changing priorities and events. One method to do this is to set aside time each day that is open on your schedule. This enables you to be flexible when events change or unexpected tasks crop up – and this happens daily in many environments.

Beginning now, set aside time each day that is free from obligation. Then, when the unexpected happens you have the flexibility to change. If nothing happens, you can then use that free time to catch up on longer-term projects, organization or building relationships. Expect the unexpected and be able to adapt to it as easily as possible. We recommend that you set aside an hour each morning and an hour mid-afternoon to be free. Having this time available for the unexpected will reduce your stress considerably and make you much more flexible and responsive.

I leave contingency time in my schedule to deal with "the unexpected."

Your Score: 1 (strongly disagree)   2 (disagree)   3 (agree)   4 (strongly agree)

Score: 3	Coaches' Recommendations

This is a good score for this item, but you can improve. We recommend that you set aside time each day that is free from any obligations. Be rigid in saving this time so that when the unexpected occurs you are able to quickly adjust your schedule with minimal impact on other tasks or events.

If you do not use this time to deal with the unexpected, it is free time that you can work on longer-term projects, organization, and building relationships with customers or your direct reports.

Score: 4	Coaches' Recommendations

You feel you do an excellent job dealing with the unexpected. Continue to model this behavior and coach others who may need tools to be able to be more flexible with their time. In today's busy world you must build time into your schedule that is free from obligation. This enables you to be more flexible when the unexpected occurs. Your goal is to be able to handle unexpected problems or events with minimal impact on your other responsibilities. Since you do this well, take it upon yourself to coach others to do well in this area.

Having a team that is adaptable to changing conditions and responsibilities will lower the stress level across the organization.

I leave contingency time in my schedule to deal with "the unexpected."

List the development steps you will take to improve in this item.

1.

2.

3.

4.

Other Notes:

I say "no" when asked to do tasks that are not in my area of responsibility when appropriate.

Sometimes you just have to say no! You have a set of responsibilities that consume much of your time. Fulfilling commitments to others is important, so if you say "yes" you are committed to fulfilling the obligation. In particular, you should not commit to doing tasks that are not in your area of responsibility or expertise. You could be setting yourself up for failure while also cutting into your time to complete your own work.

When saying no, it helps to provide an explanation. If you are too busy trying to fulfill your own responsibilities, just say so – that is usually a good enough response.

> ### *Coaches' Challenge*
>
> *How hard is it for you to say no? Think about how you feel when you are asked to do something, you don't have the time, but you say you will do it anyway. You may cut corners on quality. You may feel bitter toward the person who asked you to do the task. How often do you want to say no but don't?*

On the next two pages, circle the score you gave yourself for this statement in the "Know Your Heading" exercise. Then, read the Coaches' Recommendations for your score.

"A man who dares to waste one hour of life has not discovered the value of life."
- Charles Darwin

I say "no" when asked to do tasks that are not in my area of responsibility when appropriate.

Your Score: 1 (strongly disagree)   2 (disagree)   3 (agree)   4 (strongly agree)

Score: 1	Coaches' Recommendations

Some people just can't say no and apparently you are one of them. Think of the impact this has had on you and your productivity. Has your reluctance to say no caused you to get behind in your own work? Most likely at times it has and you need to better discern when to say yes and when to say no.

Beginning today, seriously assess whether you should fulfill each task or request that comes from others. Consider the time you have available and the impact it would have if you agreed to take on the task. In particular, don't hesitate to say no to tasks that are not in your area of responsibility. Taking on tasks that are not in your responsibility or area of expertise can often lead to disastrous results. You may not have the capability or experience to do what is asked and the end product can be poor quality, and this reflects on you. Help manage your time better by thinking about your commitments and saying no when appropriate.

Score: 2	Coaches' Recommendations

It is hard to say no, particularly when you are trying to be a team player and contribute to the success of the organization. But, think of the negative consequences when you commit to doing tasks outside your area of responsibility or expertise. If you do this often you will not have the time available to complete your tasks.

Saying no is important at times, but it should also come with an explanation. Don't say no simply to get out of doing something. If you need to say no to an assignment because you do not have the time or the expertise, tell the requester. Typically, people will understand why you cannot fulfill every request.

I say "no" when asked to do tasks that are not in my area of responsibility when appropriate.

Your Score: 1 (strongly disagree) 2 (disagree) 3 (agree) 4 (strongly agree)

Score: 3	Coaches' Recommendations

You think you do a good job saying no to requests that are not in your area of responsibility or expertise. Continue to model this behavior. However, don't say no every time. You are a team player and part of your responsibility is to help others. Effective leaders can quickly discern whether they have the time and ability to help in areas outside their responsibility.

As a leader, encourage others to focus on their areas of responsibility before asking others to help. This is not to discourage team efforts, but rather to foster self-reliance and minimize abuses of people's time.

Score: 4	Coaches' Recommendations

Continue to model this excellent behavior. As an effective leader you know when to say no. If you have peers or direct reports who have difficulty in this area, coach them to understand the impact if they take on tasks outside their area of responsibility, especially when their time is limited.

Also, watch out for the person who is constantly asking others to do things for them. Are they carrying their own weight? If someone is abusing others' time in this way, be sure to give them feedback and stress the importance of doing their job without the help of others (unless it is truly needed).

I say "no" when asked to do tasks that are not in my area of responsibility when appropriate.

List the development steps you will take to improve in this item.

1.

2.

3.

4.

Other Notes:

I do not get distracted from the tasks I am working on.

We all get distracted at times; but some seem to invite the distractions. In today's world there are many distractions and we don't have to go far to get them. Multi-tasking is supposedly a big plus. However, as the quote below illustrates, trying to do two things at once is to do neither. You must be "present in the moment" and concentrate to do the best you can with the task at hand. Common distractions such as online gaming, instant messaging, e-mail and social media sites detract from concentration and quality of work.

Identify what is distracting you and take steps to minimize this disruption from what you should be doing. The development recommendations for this item give you ideas on how to control distractions.

Coaches' Challenge

What are your major distractions? Is it interruptions? Is it checking Facebook frequently throughout the day? Is it checking e-mail too frequently. List your most prevalent distractions.

On the next two pages, circle the score you gave yourself for this statement in the "Know Your Heading" exercise. Then, read the Coaches' Recommendations for your score.

"To do two things at once is to do neither."
- Publius Syrus

I do not get distracted from the tasks I am working on.

Your Score: 1 (strongly disagree) 2 (disagree) 3 (agree) 4 (strongly agree)

Score: 1	Coaches' Recommendations

The first step to improve in this area is to keep track of how you are distracted throughout the day. Begin listing each distraction as it occurs – other people, computer games, e-mail alerts, text messages. Even if the distraction is momentary, it kills your concentration. List every distraction, no matter how much time it consumes. Once you have listed your distractions, set some rules to govern your behaviors and stick with them.

For example, instead of keeping your e-mail open all day, check it two or three times a day at a scheduled time. Another step may be to turn the text messaging off on your phone while you are working. If others are distracting you, put a "Do Not Disturb" sign on your door or in your work area.

Score: 2	Coaches' Recommendations

Distractions ruin your concentration and make it very difficult to get anything accomplished. We are faced with distractions throughout the day, every day. It is how they are handled that determine whether they have an impact on our time or not. Your first step is to identify the distractions that hinder you the most – e-mail, other people, text messaging, a wandering mind.

Then, set some ground rules on your behavior. Pledge, for example, to only check e-mail three times a day or turn off your text messaging when you are working. Whatever distractions are prevalent and impacting your concentration or time determine what rule you should apply. It is up to you, however, to follow the rules and become more focused and efficient in what you do.

I do not get distracted from the tasks I am working on.

Your Score: 1 (strongly disagree) 2 (disagree) 3 (agree) 4 (strongly agree)

Score: 3	Coaches' Recommendations

This is a good score for this item, but you feel you are distracted at times. Take a few moments and think about what distracts you and ruins your concentration or consumes your time. If you can think of specific instances, establish a rule you will follow that reminds you to avoid that behavior.

As a leader you need to set the example for concentration and focus on your tasks. In particular, you should not engage in time wasting activities such as Facebook or other social media when you are at work

Score: 4	Coaches' Recommendations

This is an excellent score for this item. Continue to model this behavior. Be aware of others on your team that may need coaching or feedback to identify that they have a problem in this area. In particular, as a leader you should try to give everyone a level of privacy and quiet in their workplace to enable them to concentrate. You can talk with your team and identify ways they are distracted and take active steps to minimize the distractions. For example, if some people are bothered by the noise in the office, you may consider allowing them to wear headphones to mask the noise.

I do not get distracted from the tasks I am working on.

List the development steps you will take to improve in this item.

1.

2.

3.

4.

Other Notes:

I delegate time-consuming tasks when appropriate.

Delegation can be a huge help in managing your time. You do not need to do everything and, if you feel you must, there probably is a trust issue between you and your team. You should be delegating tasks as much as possible so you can devote your time to tasks and efforts only you can do. Even if you feel it will take more time to delegate than to actually do the task, you should still delegate as many tasks as possible. It empowers your team members and the cumulative amount of time you have saved will be able to be devoted to more important tasks.

To delegate also implies that you trust other people to do quality work as well as you can in that area. It is a great motivator to others when you delegate tasks to them. Ensure, however, that you are delegating equitably and that the people have the time to devote to the task without impeding their other work.

Coaches' Challenge

Do you have difficulty delegating? Many of us do. What are the obstacles keeping you from delegating tasks? In many cases we feel that if we want something done right, we need to do it ourselves. We fail to realize that others may be able to do something just as well and in less time; therefore, freeing us to do other tasks that require our attention.

On the next two pages, circle the score you gave yourself for this statement in the "Know Your Heading" exercise. Then, read the Coaches' Recommendations for your score.

"One cannot manage too many affairs: like pumpkins in the water,
one pops up while you try to hold down the other."
                                                            - Chinese Proverb

148

I delegate time-consuming tasks when appropriate.

Your Score: 1 (strongly disagree) 2 (disagree) 3 (agree) 4 (strongly agree)

Score: 1	Coaches' Recommendations

Why don't you delegate more tasks that are consuming your time? This is an important question for you to analyze. In many cases, people feel they are the only one who can do something; therefore, they cannot delegate it. If you do not feel your team can step up to a task, perhaps you should be focusing on developing their skills.

Review all that tasks that are "on your plate." Decide what can be delegated and what cannot. Be objective and honest with yourself. Review the skill set of each member of your team. Next, identify one of your tasks that can be delegated to each team member. Be clear on your expectations and then give them room to complete the tasks. You may be surprised at how well it goes. Moving forward, review your task list frequently and delegate as much as possible, especially time-consuming tasks that can be done by others.

Score: 2	Coaches' Recommendations

Delegation is difficult for many leaders. It requires trust and confidence in your team members. You feel you have some issues here and do not delegate enough. We recommend you give serious thought to the benefits of delegating time-consuming tasks. Not only will it give you more time to focus on what you need to do, it will also empower your team members and improve their confidence in themselves.

Identify tasks on your list that you can delegate and then assign them to team members. Be clear on your expectations of them and be available for questions and guidance. Otherwise, step back and let them perform. This opportunity also gives your team members the opportunity to develop and grow in their job. Be careful that you do not delegate too much to the person you perceive as your best employee; spread the wealth. Also, be aware of what your employee workloads are and do not delegate tasks that will stretch them too thin.

I delegate time-consuming tasks when appropriate.

Your Score: 1 (strongly disagree) 2 (disagree) 3 (agree) 4 (strongly agree)

Score: 3	Coaches' Recommendations

This is a good score for this item and we recommend you continue to delegate your time consuming tasks as much as possible. If you want to improve in this area, focus on delegating tasks that will "stretch" the abilities of your team members and use it as a learning experience for them. Always be clear with them on your expectations.

Your main purpose in delegating, however, should be to give yourself more time to do what is most important in your allotted schedule.

Score: 4	Coaches' Recommendations

This is a very good score for this item and we recommend continuing to model this behavior. As a leader, look at your peers and see if any other leaders have difficulty delegating. If so, offer to coach them to be better in this area. For example, you can review their to-do list and recommend certain tasks that can be delegated. If they feel they cannot delegate because they do not have confidence in their team, recommend that they delegate some simple tasks to build up their team members' confidence in themselves and also the leader's confidence in them.

I delegate time-consuming tasks when appropriate.

List the development steps you will take to improve in this item.

1.

2.

3.

4.

Other Notes:

I use goals, plans and measures to guide my efforts.

What do goals, plans and measures have to do with time management? A lot! By having clear goals and a plan to attain these goals you save time. Being able to measure progress helps you plan your time for the future. If you don't have these tools in place you stand a greater risk of doing a lot of "rework" and possibly even needing to start over after you thought you were finished.

The effective leader does not start a project until it has been planned. Setting goals and developing the plan to achieve them helps every project be successful – in the least amount of time.

Coaches' Challenge

How much "rework" do you do? Have you ever gotten half done with a project and realized you had no idea how time consuming and difficult it would be?

Think about how you do projects. Do you have goals, plans and measures that you use to guide your work? Or, do you simply jump into things and work-work-work toward finishing, with no plan in mind?

On the next two pages, circle the score you gave yourself for this statement in the "Know Your Heading" exercise. Then, read the Coaches' Recommendations for your score.

"While we are postponing, life speeds by."
- Seneca

I use goals, plans and measures to guide my efforts.

Your Score: 1 (strongly disagree) 2 (disagree) 3 (agree) 4 (strongly agree)

Score: 1	Coaches' Recommendations

Starting now, do not begin a project or initiative until you have set the goals for the project, created a plan for completion, and set measures to gauge your progress toward completion. This will save you significant time and prevent rework. Project planning is critical toward creating the best results possible in the least amount of time.

Think about how you do things now. Are you disorganized? Do you know how much time each project will take? Do you know if you are going in the right direction? Do you know what resources you need to complete each project?

Tell yourself that you will plan each project from this point forward. You will not only have a plan but clear goals you can communicate with others. You will also have a way to measure progress toward the goals. Do you think if you do so you will save a significant amount of time? As coaches we know from experience that you will.

Score: 2	Coaches' Recommendations

It is good that you recognize that you need improvement in this area. Having goals, plans and measures not only will save you time but will increase the probability of success on each project. As a first step, look at some past projects and analyze how much time you could have saved if you had planned properly. What could you have done differently?

Next, set the goals, plans and measures for a project you are now beginning. Determine how you will measure progress. As you begin the project under this new method, measure your time spent and compare with similar projects you struggled with in the past.

As a leader you need to set the example in this area and expect each of your teams to use goals, plans and measures to complete projects in the shortest time possible with the best results.

I use goals, plans and measures to guide my efforts.

Your Score: 1 (strongly disagree) 2 (disagree) 3 (agree) 4 (strongly agree)

Score: 3	Coaches' Recommendations

This is a good score for this item, but you realize that you could improve. In the future, take the time to set goals for each project and develop a plan with measures to gauge your progress. As a leader you need to be a model in this area and coach your team members in project management techniques. If you practice these techniques yourself it will be easier for your team to understand why you require them to do the same.

Some people are hesitant to put the time into developing goals, plans and measures for their projects. They think it takes too much time upfront and they could be doing the actual work. When this happens, however, there is often much rework as time goes on – and this consumes significant time.

Score: 4	Coaches' Recommendations

This is an excellent score for this item and we applaud your dedication to doing things right! Now, your responsibility as a leader is to institutionalize project management techniques across the organization. Are there peers or other teams that are not aware of the importance of setting goals, plans and measures? If so, consider how you can convince them of how these processes save time, money and increase quality.

Perhaps your teams need project management training. In our coaching practice we see many young teams that have a strong desire to do things right but just don't know how because they have not been exposed to project management techniques. If your organization engages in a lot of projects, consider this type of training for your entire team.

I use goals, plans and measures to guide my efforts.

List the development steps you will take to improve in this item.

1.

2.

3.

4.

Other Notes:

I do not "make work."

People often make work, and justify doing so, when they are avoiding a difficult task or tasks they don't enjoy. The time spent on "make work" tasks is wasted time. Many people get creative when they are avoiding a difficult task. They may say, "Now is the time I need to clean and organize my office!" Meanwhile, the difficult, and usually important task goes unattended.

Effective leaders tackle their most difficult tasks first. Getting those tasks completed first gives them more time and less stress to deal with other things.

> ### *Coaches' Challenge*
>
> *Yes, some people make work. Do you? You make work if you do something you may enjoy doing at the expense of something you should be doing. People often make work to avoid doing a difficult task. When have you engaged in this behavior and what could you do to prevent it in the future?*

On the next two pages, circle the score you gave yourself for this statement in the "Know Your Heading" exercise. Then, read the Coaches' Recommendations for your score.

"A wise person does at once what a fool does at last.
Both do the same thing; only at different times."
- Baltasar Gracian

I do not "make work."

Your Score: 1 (strongly disagree)   2 (disagree)   3 (agree)   4 (strongly agree)

Score: 1	Coaches' Recommendations

Why do you "make work?" Typically we make work to avoid doing tasks that are difficult or not very interesting. Beginning today, prioritize your tasks on your "to-do" list according to their importance (not what you may want the priority to be). Then, focus on the highest priority items, even if they are the most difficult tasks.

Avoiding difficult or unpleasant tasks adds stress because we know we should be focusing on completing them. Do yourself a favor and don't make work to avoid difficult tasks. As hard as it may sound, do the difficult tasks first and develop this habit. It will lower your stress level and also enable you to get the most important tasks completed.

Score: 2	Coaches' Recommendations

It is hard to believe that some people "make work." Your score for this item indicates you sometimes do this; probably to avoid difficult or unpleasant tasks. Because you recognize that you make work, we suspect you understand why you do so. We recommend that you review your priority list every day and focus on getting the highest priority tasks completed first, regardless of whether they are difficult or not.

Sometimes, however, you may not have the concentration or energy to do the highest priority and most difficult tasks. It may not be the best time of day or you are not at your peak performance level. In that case, take some time (not long) to do other tasks but first schedule when you will begin the more difficult task. You may say to yourself, "OK, I am tired right now and not thinking clearly. Therefore, I will work on cleaning up my files and then take a short walk. I will get back on track doing my difficult tasks in one hour."

I do not "make work."

Your Score: 1 (strongly disagree)   2 (disagree)   3 (agree)   4 (strongly agree)

Score: 3	Coaches' Recommendations

Your score for this item indicates you normally do well and address difficult tasks as your priority. However, you feel you could improve in this area. Why do you sometimes "make work?" If you are avoiding difficult tasks, use your priority list to guide what you should be doing. You can also use your daily schedule to set aside specific time to focus on the difficult or unpleasant tasks.

Making extra work is often not evident to others, but they will model your behavior if they know you are avoiding a difficult or unpleasant task. Set the model in this area and demonstrate to your team that you are not hesitant to tackle the difficult tasks.

Score: 4	Coaches' Recommendations

This is an excellent score for this item and we recommend you continue to model this behavior. You may observe others, especially direct reports, who avoid doing difficult tasks. They seem to always have something going on that is more important. If this is the case, take the time to coach them on how to focus on their priority list. Help uncover their fears about doing the difficult tasks. You may need to work with them for a period of time to give them confidence in doing difficult tasks. The message you want to convey to those who have this problem is that the only way the difficult or unpleasant tasks will go away is to do the work and get them out of the way.

I do not "make work."

List the development steps you will take to improve in this item.

1.

2.

3.

4.

Other Notes:

I use a manageable to-do list focusing on what needs to be done.

Having an effective "to-do" list is the most critical time management tool. Those who use a list that works for them are guided to do what needs to be done by the list. At a minimum, the to-do list should identify all the tasks that need to be accomplished and include some type of prioritization method so that the most important tasks rise to the top.

An effective list must be managed. By that we mean that it must be used, analyzed and revised to fit the current circumstances. An unimportant task may be on your list for a long time, rolling over from day-to-day until eventually you have the time available to complete it. On the other hand, an important task may be on your list a short period of time. Because of its priority you focus your attention on getting it done.

Please review our section on "to-do" lists on page 44 for various options for using an effective list.

Coaches' Challenge

How could you improve your to-do list? What system do you use? Is it effective? Do you use it to guide what you focus on each day? Do you get "hung up" on maintaining the list as opposed to doing what is on the list?

On the next two pages, circle the score you gave yourself for this statement in the "Know Your Heading" exercise. Then, read the Coaches' Recommendations for your score.

"The great dividing line between success and failure can be expressed in six words: "I did not have the time.""

- Franklin Field

I use a manageable to-do list focusing on what needs to be done.

Your Score: 1 (strongly disagree) 2 (disagree) 3 (agree) 4 (strongly agree)

Score: 1	Coaches' Recommendations

Your "to-do" list isn't working for you. Time to change! Perhaps you don't have a list. Or, you may not be using it effectively. We recommend you read the section of this workbook on to-do lists – see page 44.

A to do list can be your most effective time management tool. Carrying it around "in your head" typically does not work. You need something tangible that you can hold, study and revise according to circumstances. The list should not be elaborate but it should capture all the tasks you need to do and prioritize them into at least three categories – urgent and important; important but not urgent; and not important and not urgent (for example – you may call the categories something else).

Your list should be the first thing you look at each morning when arriving at work. A quick review will show you where your focus should be for the upcoming day. Check it again throughout the day. Add new tasks and reprioritize as necessary. Make to-do list effectiveness a priority.

Score: 2	Coaches' Recommendations

You feel you need to improve in how you use your "to-do" list and we urge you to do so immediately. An effective list that prioritizes your tasks can be your best time management tool. Please review our section on to do lists on page 44 to get ideas on other systems that may work better for you.

Your list should be the first thing you look at each morning. A quick review will show you where your focus should be for the upcoming day. Check it again throughout the day. Add new tasks and reprioritize as necessary.

I use a manageable to-do list focusing on what needs to be done.

Your Score: 1 (strongly disagree) 2 (disagree) 3 (agree) 4 (strongly agree)

Score: 3	Coaches' Recommendations

This is a good score for this item but you may feel you could be more effective in managing your to-do list. Please review the section in this workbook on to-do lists on page 44. This section may give you ideas on how to be more effective or to choose a system that works best for you.

A to-do list should be used frequently throughout the day to help you stay on track with your priorities. What difficulties do you have in managing your to-do list? Some people become "slaves" to their list and spend too much time maintaining the list. Your list should be simple enough to maintain in a few minutes each day.

Score: 4	Coaches' Recommendations

This is an excellent score for this item and clearly your to-do list is working well for you. Is there anyone in your organization who does not keep a to-do list? If so, you may want to share your method with them. Also, be aware if anyone becomes too focused on maintaining their list and growing it, as opposed to others who are striving to make their list smaller. Some people spend their time thinking of every possible task to add to their list – almost as if they are creating a "badge of honor" for having the biggest list. If you have a colleague or direct report who takes this attitude, give them feedback on how to be more effective in this area.

I use a manageable to-do list focusing on what needs to be done.

List the development steps you will take to improve in this item.

1.

2.

3.

4.

Other Notes:

I engage in physical activity every day.

We included this item as part of time management because it directly relates to the quality of the time you spend at work. If you engage in regular physical activity you will be more alert and focused on your work. In addition, we feel that physical activity should be part of your quest to ensure that you have good work-life balance.

Many people find that their clearest thinking, and thus planning and problem solving, occurs when being engaged in physical activity. This is one time when you can truly "multi-task" without negatively affecting the quality of your work.

> ### *Coaches' Challenge*
>
> *What types of physical activity do you engage in daily? If you aren't doing anything physical each day, why not? The time you spend walking or working out is time well spent. Studies have shown that those who engage in physical activity are more alert, energized and focused when they go back to work. List your options for physical activity.*

On the next two pages, circle the score you gave yourself for this statement in the "Know Your Heading" exercise. Then, read the Coaches' Recommendations for your score.

"You will never "find" time for anything. If you want time, you must make it."
- Charles Bruxton

I engage in physical activity every day.

Your Score: 1 (strongly disagree) 2 (disagree) 3 (agree) 4 (strongly agree)

Score: 1	Coaches' Recommendations

The typical excuse for those who do not engage in regular physical activity is that they do not have enough time. Well, make time – it will pay off in the long run because you will be more engaged in your work and more focused. The time spent in physical activity can often be used to think through issues and problems.

List the types of physical activity you enjoy. Start slowly by committing to do something each day for 15 minutes. Then, increase your time over the next few weeks. Try to schedule your activity at the same time each day. This will help you develop a habit that over time will be less likely to be broken.

List the benefits, both physical and mental, that you will gain by your physical activity. When you don't feel inclined to take the time for physical activity, review your benefits list.

Score: 2	Coaches' Recommendations

You feel you need to improve in this area and we couldn't agree more! Physical activity each day will not only bring you physical benefits but also help sharpen your mind and your focus as you work. Your first step is to think about your options. What physical activities do you enjoy? What is the best time of the day to commit to physical activity?

Take the steps to begin immediately and develop a habit of committing the time to physical activity each day. As soon as you do it and maintain your schedule, the sooner you will develop the habit. Be careful to pace yourself in the beginning. Perhaps you begin with 15 minutes of activity and then increase the time commitment each week until you are spending 30 – 45 minutes each day on physical activity.

I engage in physical activity every day.

Your Score: 1 (strongly disagree) 2 (disagree) 3 (agree) 4 (strongly agree)

Score: 3	Coaches' Recommendations

You scored well for this item but perhaps you think you can do better. A common problem is that people commit to physical activity but then allow obstacles to keep them from following through. Things may go well for a few weeks, but when a big deadline is approaching it is easy to put off the physical activity to focus on the deadline. Then, it is difficult to get back to the physical activity routine.

We recommend that you commit to a schedule of physical activity each day at a time that works best for you. Perhaps you need to get up a little earlier each day. Or, you firmly commit to being active during your lunch time. The more you stick to the same routine the earlier the physical activity will become a habit that is hard to break. When faced with obstacles or competing priorities, remind yourself of the benefits of the physical activity.

Score: 4	Coaches' Recommendations

This is an excellent score and we encourage you to continue to engage in daily physical activity. Not only are you benefitting yourself but you are setting a good example for others. Some who see you working out, walking or running may question your commitment to work. But, they will shortly see the benefits that you bring to the table due to your physical activity – better focus, more energy and a better attitude.

Use your leadership and influencing skills to get others involved in physical activities. Understand, however, that not all may be interested in the same activities as you or have the same capabilities. Can your organization provide the facilities needed to encourage physical fitness such as changing rooms, showers or membership in a local health club?

I engage in physical activity every day.

List the development steps you will take to improve in this item.

1.

2.

3.

4.

Other Notes:

I only work outside normal hours when necessary.

You should normally be able to get your work done during scheduled work hours. This is not always the case because deadlines may necessitate extra time or an unexpected problem may need solved. But, in the normal course of things, you should be able to finish your work during scheduled hours. If not, you need to analyze the situation and understand why. If you consistently have too much work to complete in your scheduled time, think about getting more help or delegate more tasks.

Work-life balance is important and you should minimize the amount of work you do outside normal hours.

Coaches' Challenge

Some people make it a habit to work at home. They justify it by saying they have fewer interruptions and get more done. Do you take work home often? What is your excuse? If you are unable to accomplish things at work, why not? Perhaps you are providing an unacceptable solution to another problem, such as being distracted at work.

On the next two pages, circle the score you gave yourself for this statement in the "Know Your Heading" exercise. Then, read the Coaches' Recommendations for your score.

"Your greatest resource is your time."
- Brian Tracy

I only work outside normal hours when necessary.

Your Score: 1 (strongly disagree)   2 (disagree)   3 (agree)   4 (strongly agree)

Score: 1	Coaches' Recommendations

At least you recognize that you are doing too much work outside of normal work hours. Do you understand that consistently doing work outside normal hours is a very bad habit that you must learn to control? What are the impacts on your personal life and your professional life if you consistently work outside normal hours?

What are the reasons you are not getting your work done in the allotted time? Your initial focus should be on identifying the reasons and then addressing them. Do you need to delegate more? Are you suffering from too many distractions at work? Are you working extra hours to avoid other personal issues? Once you have identified the reasons, immediately take steps to fix the situation. Set a rule: you will only work beyond normal hours if there is a serious deadline looming or a major problem to be solved – one that cannot wait until the next day. You may need an "accountability partner" who will remind you when it is time to leave and to ensure that you are not taking work with you.

Score: 2	Coaches' Recommendations

Your first step is to consider why you are working so much beyond normal work hours. There may be many reasons why you need the extra time and identifying those reasons is the first step toward taking action to improve. Consider, however, that you may be rationalizing your extra work time to avoid other problems. If that is the case, we encourage you to get help to resolve your issues.

Working beyond normal hours sets a bad example for others. Your direct reports may feel they need to do the same, and this could have a serious negative effect for them in their personal life, and leave them stressed and tired during normal work hours.

I only work outside normal hours when necessary.

Your Score: 1 (strongly disagree) 2 (disagree) 3 (agree) 4 (strongly agree)

Score: 3	**Coaches' Recommendations**

This is a good score for this item; however, we suspect that you want to improve. Are there times you take work home when you don't really need to do so? If this is the case, why? You should do your best to minimize the work you do outside normal hours. As a leader, this sets a good example for others. If, however, you are taking too much work home consistently, perhaps you are not delegating enough or you are distracted at work. Take steps to correct this if either case fits you.

If you consistently take work home because there is too much to do, and you cannot delegate the work, consider that you may need more help or that the organization is not structured right – putting too much on you when the work and responsibilities are not shared equitably.

Analyze the situation and if you need to make adjustments, do so. Sometimes it is necessary to do work outside normal hours, just be cautious that it does not become a habit.

Score: 4	**Coaches' Recommendations**

This is an excellent score for this item and you set a good example for others. As a leader you need to ensure that the work you assign is equitable and your direct reports are able to complete their tasks in normal work hours. Yes, they may need to work extra at times; however, this should not be the norm. If someone on your team does not do well in this area, talk with them to understand why they consistently are working outside normal hours. If you can help them understand why they do so you are in a position that you can offer solutions.

I only work outside normal hours when necessary.

List the development steps you will take to improve in this item.

1.

2.

3.

4.

Other Notes:

I set aside time for planning and scheduling.

Planning and scheduling are excellent time management tools that every effective leader should use. Often, however, people do not take the time to plan their projects or initiatives. The also don't take the time to develop a schedule that will ensure that they get done what is needed. The rationalization is that there is not enough time to plan and schedule tasks. In reality, adequate planning and scheduling save time in the long run, and also lead to better results.

Coaches' Challenge

Do you do adequate planning and scheduling? Or, do you jump right into a project and start moving forward with what needs to be done? There are cases where you should jump right in, but in most cases you will be better off planning your activities and building a schedule that works for you. Planning and scheduling are excellent time management skills that save you much time in the long run.

On the next two pages, circle the score you gave yourself for this statement in the "Know Your Heading" exercise. Then, read the Coaches' Recommendations for your score.

"A year from now you will wish you had started today."
- Karen Lamb

I set aside time for planning and scheduling.

Your Score: 1 (strongly disagree) 2 (disagree) 3 (agree) 4 (strongly agree)

Score: 1	Coaches' Recommendations

Thank you for recognizing and admitting that you do not set aside time for planning and scheduling. Awareness is the first step toward improvement. Would you agree that planning and scheduling will save time in the long run? If so, you are ready for improvement. We recommend, as a first step, that you take fifteen minutes each day to plan and schedule your activities for the day.

Your next step is to look more long term and plan and schedule the work for the various projects and initiatives you may have on your plate. Think about what needs to be done and how much time it will take to complete. Determine what resources are needed and schedule them to align with when they are needed. Talk to others who have completed similar projects. Find out what they needed and how much time each task took. This gives you the data needed to create a workable plan and effective schedule. Don't jump into things anymore – take the time to plan and schedule.

Score: 2	Coaches' Recommendations

You want to improve in this area, but it will take an investment of time. Planning takes time but the return on the investment will be more time in the future. Take the time each day to plan your activities. Schedule the work you are going to do throughout the day.

Before you begin a new project, plan what needs to be done. Talk to others and estimate how much time each task will take and identify the resource you will need. Create a workable schedule that can be integrated into your daily schedule.

Don't go through another day or begin another project without adequate planning and scheduling.

I set aside time for planning and scheduling.

Your Score: 1 (strongly disagree) 2 (disagree) 3 (agree) 4 (strongly agree)

Score: 3	Coaches' Recommendations

This is a good score for this item but likely you don't plan or schedule your work all the time. Are we right in assuming you know the benefits of planning and scheduling? If so, what is keeping you from doing a daily schedule and a project plan for initiatives? There may be times when you need to immediately begin a task, one that you have done repeatedly for a long time, and you don't need to plan for it. But if it comes up it surely has an impact on your schedule. Take the time to evaluate the impacts to your schedule and make the adjustments accordingly.

Do your best to plan well and use a daily schedule to outline your activities. Planning and scheduling will save much time in the long run.

Score: 4	Coaches' Recommendations

This is an excellent score for this item and we recommend that you continue to model this behavior. Insist that your direct reports or project managers create plans for their projects or initiatives. Help them schedule their new work around other tasks that they are doing. If any have difficulty prioritizing, step up and give them guidance and feedback.

Meantime, continue to plan each day. Use your schedule to drive the activities you are working on.

I set aside time for planning and scheduling.

List the development steps you will take to improve in this item.

1.

2.

3.

4.

Other Notes:

I reward myself after an achievement.

Typically, achievements take time and commitment. Often you are required to put in extra time and focus intently on what needs to be done. Other tasks are put aside so that you can achieve the initiative at hand. It is important that you reward yourself after achieving a goal; and typically this includes taking compensatory time.

After giving a great effort you need "recharged" with energy and motivation. It is difficult to jump right into another project or initiative. If you continue to do so you will eventually get burnt out and not do your best work. Your attitude will be damaged as well. Other parts of your life may suffer.

Coaches' Challenge

Think of past achievements. What did you do to reward yourself after completion? Did you jump right into the next project? What kinds of "rewards" are important to you after you complete a major project or accomplish an achievement?

On the next two pages, circle the score you gave yourself for this statement in the "Know Your Heading" exercise. Then, read the Coaches' Recommendations for your score.

"Ordinary people think merely of spending time. Great people think of using it."
- Unknown

I reward myself after an achievement.

Your Score: 1 (strongly disagree) 2 (disagree) 3 (agree) 4 (strongly agree)

Score: 1	Coaches' Recommendations

Rewards are important, even self rewards you give yourself after an achievement. We work hard for many reasons but it should not be the end all. Having a "life" is important to each of us. When you work hard you deserve a reward. What are the obstacles that prevent you from rewarding yourself when you achieve your goals?

There may be times that you cannot reward yourself immediately with extra time off due to additional demands. If that is the case, look forward and determine when you can take the time. Put it on your schedule and do not let other projects or demands interfere. It is too easy to put things off if we don't make the commitment. You committed yourself to achieve the goal or complete the project; you can also commit to taking care of yourself.

Score: 2	Coaches' Recommendations

You have the responsibility, not the organization, to yourself to ensure that you are rewarded in whatever works best for you. If you put in extra hours to achieve your goals, take extra time off whenever possible.

There may be times that you cannot reward yourself immediately with time off due to additional demands. If that is the case, look forward and determine when you can take the time. Put it on your schedule and do not let other projects or demands interfere. It is too easy to put things off if we don't make the commitment. You committed yourself to achieve the goal or complete the project; you can also commit yourself to taking care of yourself.

I reward myself after an achievement.

Your Score: 1 (strongly disagree) 2 (disagree) 3 (agree) 4 (strongly agree)

Score: 3	Coaches' Recommendations

This is a good score for this item and we are glad you reward yourself after achieving a goal. Continue to model this behavior. It is important to set the example for achieving a good work-life balance and keeping your professional life in perspective.

There may be times you cannot reward yourself immediately with time off due to additional demands. If that is the case, look forward and determine when you can take the time. Put it on your schedule and do not let other projects or demands interfere. It is too easy to put things off if we don't make the commitment. You committed yourself to achieve the goal or complete the project; you can also commit yourself to taking care of yourself.

Score: 4	Coaches' Recommendations

This is excellent behavior to model and we applaud you for achieving a good balance in this area. As a leader, you may have to insist that others follow your lead. In particular, you have a responsibility to your direct reports to monitor their stress level and ability to move from one major effort to another. Some may need time off or other reward, while others do not. Be observant of the level of strain that people feel when faced with multiple high priority projects. Insist that your team members take care of themselves when they push through a major effort.

I reward myself after an achievement.

List the development steps you will take to improve in this item.

1.

2.

3.

4.

Other Notes:

I am "present in the moment" whether at work or not at work.

Being "present in the moment" means that you are able to give your full attention to what you are doing at the moment. Your mind is not wandering and you are not concerned about other things in your professional or personal world. This ability to concentrate enables you to make better decision, be more productive, and have greater insight into the problems that face you.

> ### Coaches' Challenge
>
> *Does your mind wander when you are working? Does it wander back to work issues when you are at home? The best leaders are able to compartmentalize and focus their attention on what is important at the moment.*

On the next two pages, circle the score you gave yourself for this statement in the "Know Your Heading" exercise. Then, read the Coaches' Recommendations for your score.

"Those who make the worst use of their time are the first to complain of its shortness."
- Jean De La Bruyere

I am "present in the moment" whether at work or not at work.

Your Score: 1 (strongly disagree) 2 (disagree) 3 (agree) 4 (strongly agree)

Score: 1	Coaches' Recommendations

It is important to be focused on the task at hand, whether at work or in your personal life. You indicate this is a weakness. Is the problem that your mind is drifting to other topics when you are at work? Or, does your attention wander when you are at home, back to work issues? Neither situation is good. Effective leaders compartmentalize so they can focus. They know the issues in their "other world" will be there when the appropriate time comes to deal with them.

We recommend this awareness be the first step in your road to improvement. Whether you are at work or at home, concentrate on focusing on the present moment. Some leaders use a tool to help. For example, if their mind starts to wander from the moment they will pinch their fingernail into their thumb until it hurts. This is a slightly painful reminder to get in the moment. Over a short period of time behavior will improve and the tactic will not be necessary.

Score: 2	Coaches' Recommendations

It is hard to be "present in the moment," especially when worries and difficulties are occurring in one "world" or the other (or both). It is important to understand that to be most effective, either in work or in the personal world, you must be giving attention to what is occurring in the moment.

Some leaders have difficulty in the transition between the two worlds. They never effectively resolve the issues in one world when they are transitioning to the others. We recommend you use the transition time (driving home or taking a train to work, etc.) to effectively "close" the issues that are on your mind by telling yourself you will deal with each the next time you move into that world. You may not be solving your problems but you are putting them off until you can focus more clearly on them without impeding your attention on other things.

I am "present in the moment" whether at work or not at work.

Your Score: 1 (strongly disagree) 2 (disagree) 3 (agree) 4 (strongly agree)

Score: 3	Coaches' Recommendations

This is a good score for this item. To improve, practice staying in the moment by catching your mind when it wanders. Remind yourself that you are in your "work world" or your "personal world" and that you need to focus on what is at hand. Some leaders use a reminder such as pinching themselves when they catch their mind wandering.

When you are at work, your team and your tasks demand your full attention. When you are at home your family and your personal hobbies demand your attention. Continue to focus on improving in this area.

Score: 4	Coaches' Recommendations

This is an excellent score for this item and you clearly do a good job focusing on what is important at the time. Continue to be adept at compartmentalizing.

As a leader it is important that you monitor your peers and direct reports to ensure that they are present in the moment. If you observe someone who clearly is not focused on what is happening in the moment, take the time to talk with them to understand what is going on. Sometimes people who normally do well in this area face a period of difficult times and are unable to focus. Perhaps they need someone to talk with or to help them through the difficult time.

I am "present in the moment" whether at work or not at work.

List the development steps you will take to improve in this item.

1.

2.

3.

4.

Other Notes:

I monitor team members to ensure that they have balance.

You want the best performance from your team members. For that to happen, they must have a good work-life balance. It is not appropriate for you to know everything that is going on in someone's life, but you can determine if they are working too hard and not taking time off when they should. In particular, after a long or difficult project, people need to be rewarded with time so they can bring their life back into balance.

Teams that are well balanced are more productive and enjoy their work so much more than those that are pushed over the edge with the expectation that work is everything and they should give more and more and more.

Coaches' Challenge

Before you can monitor and advise your team members on work-life balance you have to have good balance yourself. Do you? Do you work all the time, only capturing brief moments when you are truly "off duty?" Or, are you able to focus on your family and outside interests when you are not working? How good do you think your balance is?

On the next two pages, circle the score you gave yourself for this statement in the "Know Your Heading" exercise. Then, read the Coaches' Recommendations for your score.

"Time is the coin of your life. It is the only coin you have, and only you can determine how it will be spent. Be careful lest you let other people spend it for you."
  - Carl Sandburg

I monitor team members to ensure that they have balance.

Your Score: 1 (strongly disagree) 2 (disagree) 3 (agree) 4 (strongly agree)

Score: 1	Coaches' Recommendations

You may disagree with this statement and feel it is not your responsibility to ensure that you team members have a good work-life balance. We believe it is your responsibility as a leader. Your team members may be working very hard and are very motivated to do a good job for you and the organization. Some team members can't always keep work in perspective and they need your guidance.

Just as important, you need to set the example in this area. Focus on getting your work-life balance in order; then, stress the importance to your team members. We recommend that you review the section on work-life balance in this workbook beginning on page 52.

Score: 2	Coaches' Recommendations

As a leader you must not only be concerned with your work-life balance, but also that of your team members. It does no one any good if you and your team are burnt out. We recommend that you set the example in this area. Take time off when needed. Learn how to be "present in the moment," and get physical exercise each day to give yourself more energy.

Monitor your team members and coach them to be better at establishing balance in their lives. Stress to them that work is important, but to achieve the best results at work they need to be good in their personal life as well. Emphasize the importance of rest and having outside interests.

Your best step to improving in this area is to set the example to your team members.

I monitor team members to ensure that they have balance.

Your Score: 1 (strongly disagree) 2 (disagree) 3 (agree) 4 (strongly agree)

Score: 3	Coaches' Recommendations

You feel you do well in this area and we commend you for your attention to your team members. It is a continuous task to monitor your team members. If someone's behavior or performance changes suddenly, talk with them to see if something has changed at work or home. Do the best you can to encourage your team members to have a good work-life balance.

It is also important that leaders monitor each other. If you have a colleague that appears to have an imbalance in their work-life spectrum, it is important that you talk with them to encourage and help them regain their balance.

Score: 4	Coaches' Recommendations

This is a very good score for this item and you need to continue to model this behavior. You should also be concerned about your peers, and if you notice an imbalance in their life, talk with them to encourage and understand what is going on. Give them tips on how to regain their balance and if the situation is serious either at home or at work, do what you can go help them resolve their issues.

I monitor team members to ensure that they have balance.

List the development steps you will take to improve in this item.

1.

2.

3.

4.

Other Notes:

I enjoy both work and non-work activities.

We are meant to enjoy our lives. It is often hard because many things are taking place both in our professional and personal lives. Most important, as leaders we are expected to demonstrate that we are happy and enjoying our job, even when we are not. After all, if we are not enjoying our work and we are "showing it on our sleeve," our team members won't be enjoying theirs either. Bad moods can be very contagious. But, so can joyful ones. As a leader, do your best to enjoy both your professional and personal life. If you aren't, do something about it.

Coaches' Challenge

Are you joyful in your work and in your off time activities? Yes, it is tough sometimes. Competing interests, doing things we may not enjoy, stress coming from all directions – but we are still expected to be happy.

It helps to think about what makes us happy. What do you enjoy about work? What do you enjoy when you are not at work? List the answers to both these questions. Keep the answers as reminders for when things get tough.

On the next two pages, circle the score you gave yourself for this statement in the "Know Your Heading" exercise. Then, read the Coaches' Recommendations for your score.

"One thing you can't recycle is wasted time."
- Unknown

I enjoy both work and non-work activities.

Your Score: 1 (strongly disagree) 2 (disagree) 3 (agree) 4 (strongly agree)

Score: 1	Coaches' Recommendations

Is this a temporary state or has your misery been going on for a while? Is it centered on work or your non-work activities? Regardless, now is the time to do something about it. If you are not finding joy in your work, what can you change to bring a sense of enjoyment? If the status quo is not working, you need to make changes.

If you are not enjoying your non-work activities - whether family, friends, or hobbies, the tendency is to throw yourself at your work. This doesn't fix the problem. You will then become unhappy at work as well. If you are not enjoying your personal life, do something about it. Perhaps you need to get counseling or talk to a strong friend. Our recommendation is to not be stuck. Take action – it is your life and you can decide whether you are going to enjoy it or not.

Score: 2	Coaches' Recommendations

What is making you unhappy? Get to the root; don't just list the surface things. If you can identify why you don't enjoy your work or your personal activities, you can do something about it. But first you need to take the time to analyze the situation to understand what is driving your unhappiness. If you are under too much stress, we recommend that you obtain our workbook titled, Stress Management – The SID Way. It will give you tips on reducing stress in both your professional and personal life.

As a leader you have a responsibility to do your best to enjoy your work. If you are not, it can be very obvious to others, including your direct reports. By the same token, if you are unhappy in your off-duty activities, it is easy to detect at work. If you are not enjoying either or both worlds, do something about it.

I enjoy both work and non-work activities.

Your Score: 1 (strongly disagree) 2 (disagree) 3 (agree) 4 (strongly agree)

Score: 3	Coaches' Recommendations

This is a good score for this item and we interpret that you find enjoyment in both your work and non-work activities – most of the time. That may be all that we can ask and you should probably continue doing things just the way you are.

However, be wary of changes that may lessen your enjoyment in either world. If something happens it can trigger you to become less joyful and you can rapidly spiral downward. At the first inkling that you are becoming unhappy in either realm, take action. Talk with trusted colleagues or friends. Determine a quick course of action that can return joy to your life.

Score: 4	Coaches' Recommendations

This is an excellent score for this item and we are glad you enjoy both your professional and personal worlds. Continue to do so.

As a leader, look around and see who is not happy. If you are able, talk with them to learn more. Perhaps it is something at work that is making them unhappy and you can do something about it – at a minimum you can explain why things may be the way they are. If it is something outside work that is making them unhappy, perhaps you can be the one person that will just listen to them without passing judgment.

I enjoy both work and non-work activities.

List the development steps you will take to improve in this item.

1.

2.

3.

4.

Other Notes:

I coach colleagues and direct reports who have time management issues.

As a leader you have a responsibility to coach your colleagues and direct reports to be more effective in time management. Of course, you must first set the example to be as effective as possible. Once you are doing your best in setting an example, you should identify who else is having a problem.

> ### Coaches' Challenge
>
> *Who on your team is having problems with time management? What should you do to help them improve? Do you feel you have a responsibility to help them change?*

On the next two pages, circle the score you gave yourself for this statement in the "Know Your Heading" exercise. Then, read the Coaches' Recommendations for your score.

"Time is the school in which we learn, time is the fire in which we burn."
Delmore Schwartz

I coach colleagues and direct reports who have time management issues.

Your Score: 1 (strongly disagree) 2 (disagree) 3 (agree) 4 (strongly agree)

Score: 1	Coaches' Recommendations

As a leader you have a responsibility to discern if any of your colleagues or direct reports have time management issues (or work-life balance issues). Your first step is to think about each colleague and direct report to assess whether you believe they have a time management or work-life balance issue. If they do, discuss with them and develop a plan of action for their improvement.

It is important, however, that you address your own issues in these areas before coaching a colleague or team member.

Score: 2	Coaches' Recommendations

As a leader you have a responsibility to discern if any of your colleagues or direct reports have time management issues (or work-life balance issues). Your first step is to think about each colleague and direct report to assess whether you believe they have a time management or work-life balance issue. If they do, discuss with them and develop a plan of action for their improvement.

It is important, however, that you address your own issues in these areas before coaching a colleague or team member.

I coach colleagues and direct reports who have time management issues.

Your Score: 1 (strongly disagree) 2 (disagree) 3 (agree) 4 (strongly agree)

Score: 3	Coaches' Recommendations

This is a good score for this item and we encourage you to continue coaching your colleagues and direct reports who may have time management or work-life balance issues. Create an environment where team members are comfortable talking with you about their problems in these areas.

Set goals with others to help them work toward managing their time better, creating a better work-life balance.

Score: 4	Coaches' Recommendations

This is an excellent score for this item and we commend you for taking an active role in helping others deal with their time management or work-life balance issues. Continue to be a model in this area. If any of your peers are not doing well in this area, take the time to coach them on how to be better at helping their team members in these areas.

I coach colleagues and direct reports who have time management issues.

List the development steps you will take to improve in this item.

1.

2.

3.

4.

Other Notes:

"Don't be fooled by the calendar. There are only as many days in the year as you make use of. One man gets only a week's value out of a year while another man gets a full year's value out of a week."

- Charles Richards

Your Development Plan

If you recall our discussion of the SID model, having a development plan is critical to improving your behaviors and skills. The development plan will guide your actions as you strive to improve and help you stay focused.

It is now time to create your development plan for Time Management. Having completed the "Know Your Heading" assessment and the Coaches' Itinerary, you should have identified specific areas you need to work on. The next page contains a template for creating the development plan.

In the left column, list the specific steps you will take. Be as descriptive as possible. The middle column is used to identify resources you may need to help improve. The right column specifies the date when you will be completed and the behavior or skill that will be improved.

Here's an example of one action:

ACTION	RESOURCES I NEED	PROGRESS CHECK DATE	COMPLETION DATE
List steps I can take to keep from procrastinating.	Time – about 1 hour to think about it. Take notes in a notebook for future reference. Help – Brainstorm ideas with James and Kelly who do a good job in this area and know me well enough to give me feedback.	5/1/11	6/30/11

"A man who dares to waste one hour of life has not discovered the value of life."
                                                    - Charles Darwin

MY DEVELOPMENT PLAN FOR TIME MANAGEMENT

ACTIONS	RESOURCES I NEED	PROGRESS CHECK DATE	COMPLETION DATE

ACTIONS	RESOURCES I NEED	PROGRESS CHECK DATE	COMPLETION DATE

Part 3 – Development Recommendations

ACTIONS	RESOURCES I NEED	PROGRESS CHECK DATE	COMPLETION DATE

ACTIONS	RESOURCES I NEED	PROGRESS CHECK DATE	COMPLETION DATE

Part 4 - Appendices

Appendix A – Takeaway Tool 1 – Time Wasters Checklist

Appendix B – Takeaway Tool 2 – Sample Meeting Agenda

Appendix C – Takeaway Tool 3 – Meeting Management Norm Statement

Appendix D – Coaches' Bookshelf

Appendix E – BenchMark Learning's 4P's Leadership Competency Model™

Appendix F – Using the SID™ Model for Organizational Improvement

Appendix A – Takeaway Tool 1

Time Wasters Checklist

Takeaway Tools are designed to help you improve your skills, behaviors and results for this competency.

Consider each of the following time wasters and check whether it is a problem for you or not. If it is a problem, create some ideas for solutions to prevent the time waster.

TIME WASTER	THIS IS A PROBLEM FOR ME	THIS IS NOT A PROBLEM FOR ME
Social Media Sites (Facebook, LinkedIn, Twitter, YouTube, etc.)		
Interruptions		
Meetings		
E-mail		
Internet		

Appendix B – Takeaway Tool 2

Sample Meeting Agenda

Takeaway Tools are designed to help you improve your skills, behaviors and results for this competency.

Most types of meetings should have a published agenda. The agenda will give participants a preview of what is to be discussed. It will also help ensure that the meeting stays on track to achieve its objectives. The following is a sample meeting agenda:

PROJECT UPDATE MEETING

AGENDA

March 12, 2011
8:00 a.m. to 9:00 a.m.

- List of Attendees   Carol

- Review of Meeting Objectives   Carol

  o Objective 1
  o Objective 2
  o Objective 3

- Project "A" Review   Kyle

  o Current status
  o Schedule
  o Upcoming events
  o Issues
  o Action items

- Project "B" Review   Daniel

  o Current status
  o Schedule
  o Upcoming events
  o Issues
  o Action items

- Project "C" Review   Paul

  o Current status
  o Schedule
  o Upcoming events
  o Issues
  o Action items

- Review of Action Items   Carol

- Parking Lot Issues Resolution (discuss if time; if not, schedule for future meeting)

- Scheduling of follow-on meetings if required

Appendix C – Takeaway Tool 3

Sample Meeting Norm Statement

Takeaway Tools are designed to help you improve your skills, behaviors and results for this competency.

A Norm Statement is an agreement by a group of people or leaders describing how things will be done. A meeting management norming statement is an excellent way to establish an organization's set of rules for meetings. The following is a sample Meeting Management Norm Statement. After the norming statement is adopted post it clearly in all meeting rooms.

As the Chancelor Corporation leadership team, we recognize the importance and value of meetings. However, we also recognize that meetings must be purposeful, managed well and have outcomes that are in alignment with the purposes for the meeting. Each meeting will have a stated (or written) purpose, schedule and written agenda. The leader of the meeting is the person who calls the meeting, regardless of "rank" or position, and has the responsibility to facilitate the meeting in the most efficient manner. Action items and parking lot issues will be published in an e-mail or document and sent to all invitees and the appropriate managers or leaders. All attendees will do their best to be prepared and on time for each meeting. If unable to attend, an invited attendee will notify the leader of the meeting.

Appendix D – Coaches' Bookshelf

Cirillo, Francesco. <u>The Pomodoro Technique</u>. San Francisco: Creative Commons. 2007.

> *This short book explains Cirillo's Pomodoro Technique of time management and productivity. We discussed this technique in the content section of this workbook. The book can be downloaded free in PDF format at <u>http://www.pomodorotechnique.com</u>*

Dodd, Pamela and Sundheim, Doug. <u>The 25 Best Time Management Tools and Techniques</u>. Peak Performance Press. 2005.

> *A no-fluff, easy-to-read compilation of the best advice from the top 20 time management books. Recommendations cover five areas: Focus, Plan, Organize, Take Action, and Learn. Short chapters cover the A to Z of time management from finding out what time means to you from prioritizing, overcoming procrastination, and managing stress and well being.*

Ferriss, Timothy. <u>The 4-Hour Workweek</u>. New York: Crown Publishers. 2007.

> *Although geared toward the budding entrepreneur, Ferriss' book has many time management nuggets that can be extremely valuable in all situations.*

Harvard Business Review. <u>Harvard Business Review on Work and Life Balance</u>. Harvard Business Press. 2001.

> *With articles ranging from an in-depth look at the "mommy-track" to perspectives on telecommuting, this book will help HR professionals and employees at all levels understand the oftentimes delicate balance between our professional and personal lives.*

Lakein, Alan. <u>How to Get Control of Your Time and Your Life</u>. Signet. 1989.

> *A famous expert reveals his professional secrets. Learn how to build your willpower, how to waste time for pleasure and profit, and how to work smarter, not harder. A practical no-nonsense guide to managing your personal and business time.*

Leland, Karen and Bailey, Keith. <u>Time Management in an Instant: 60 Ways to Make the Most of Your Day</u>. Career Press. 2008.

> *Helps the reader overcome the feeling of overload and avoid the traps that lead to an unproductive relationship with time. It offers field-tested time habits and expert advice based on the latest research. Assists the reader to better manage, create, and spend their time with more satisfaction and results.*

MacKenzie, Alec. <u>The Time Trap: The Classic Book on Time Management</u>. New York: AMACOM. 2009.

> *This all-time classic book on time management has shown countless readers how to squeeze the optimal efficiency and satisfaction out of their work day based on decades of research with businesspeople around the world. Filled with smart tactics, revealing interviews, and handy time management tools, the book has been extensively revised to cover time management challenges caused by new technologies and the Internet, and to provide technology-based solutions.*

Merrill, A Roger. <u>Life Matters: Creating a Dynamic Balance of Work, Family, Time and Money</u>. New York: McGraw Hill. 2004.

> *This thoughtful self-help manual is not a quick read, but its advice is sound and can easily be applied to daily life.*

Panella, Vince. The 26 Hour Day: How to Gain at Least Two Hours a Day with Time Control. Franklin Lakes, NJ: Career Press. 2002.

> *A book that will actually teach you how to gain two to four more profitable, productive and enjoyable hours a day at work and at home. By focusing on behaviors over organizational skills, it shatters the fallacy of traditional time management and gives you the specific skills necessary to massively leverage your time.*

Parker, Glenn and Hoffman, Robert. Meeting Excellence: 33 Tools to Lead Meetings to Get Results. Jossey-Bass. 2006.

> *A comprehensive resource that provides a wide range of ready-to-use tools that have been developed and tested by a meeting initiative within Novartis Pharmaceuticals. It is based on years of research observing team meetings, examining existing meeting documents, and conducting a number of intensive individual interviews in the U.S. and Europe. This important book offers the information and tools needed to prepare, facilitate, and follow up on all your meetings.*

Pickering, Peg and Jonathan Clark. How to Make the Most of Your Workday. Franklin Lakes, NJ: Career Press. 2002.

> *This revised and updated edition of How to Make the Most of Your Workday will help you learn how to work smarter, not harder. It is packed with tools, techniques, advice, and activities to help you permanently change the way you work and live.*

Roesch, Roberta. Time Management for Busy People. New York: McGraw-Hill. 1998.

> *Streamlined for busy people who don't have time to sit down and read a whole book, Time Management for Busy People lets you zero in on the information you need now. You'll learn mental tricks that can get you to work a few minutes early; discover how to use computers and technology to save time all day long; master the secret of doing two things at once; and even find private time for yourself. Plus you get dozens of quizzes, checklists and worksheets so you can keep track of the things you must do, the things you should do and the things you want to do.*

Silber, Lee. <u>Time Management for the Creative Person</u>. New York: Three Rivers Press. 1998.

> *Silber's goal is to create positive and lasting change by helping us organize ourselves so that we can be more, and not do more, through effective time management. Each side of our brain processes information differently, and although he stresses that there is a lot of overlap, the dominant side will be reflected in our behavior. Creativity stems from the way we see things: left-brain persons characteristically are linear thinkers who are logical, verbal and critical. Right-brain people tend to be artistic, intuitive, illogical and persuasive. The author helps us identify our dominant brain and then offers a series of stand-alone chapters on topics such as how to focus on more than one thing at a time, dealing with a tendency to be late, hundreds of time-saving tips and how to improve memory.*

Smith, J. Walker. <u>Life is Not Work, Work is Not Life: Simple Reminders for Finding Balance in a 24/7 World</u>. Wildcat Canyon Press. 2001.

> *The 20th century was defined by work: Industrialization. Downsizing. Working moms. Working couples. Daycare. Second careers. Telecommuting. 24/7. The new century brings along with it a deep-seated need to balance a strong work ethic with enjoyment of leisure time. This book of bite-sized mini essays helps to quell the frenzy that seems to have everyone working more and enjoying life less.*

Zeller, Dirk. <u>Successful Time Management for Dummies</u>. Indianapolis: Wiley. 2008.

> *This authoritative, plain-English guide shows you how to set yourself up for success, overcome common time management obstacles, and focus your efforts on your most important tasks and objectives. It explains how to determine the value of your time, provides fantastic tips on streamlining your workspace to speed up the flow, and even helps you minimize or eliminate interruptions from your workday.*

Appendix E – 4P's Leadership Competency Model™

We began our analysis of leadership competencies years ago and struggled to put a framework together that covered the necessary skills and behaviors to measure leadership abilities. Our work progressed as we designed and developed leadership assessments for university leaders from Deans to Vice Presidents to Presidents and others. At that point we began to refine our assessment of the major skills and behaviors necessary for successful and effective leadership and out of this research and work we formulated our 4P Leadership Competency Model™.

Although there are hundreds of leadership books and models of competencies, we felt a wide competency-based approach was best to fit our Self-Initiated Development model. On the next page we list these 30 leadership competencies. A workbook similar to this one is being developed for each. You can order workbooks as they are completed at www.thesidway.com.

In addition, you can complete a master self assessment that covers all 30 competencies at our website. This can be used to determine which of the competencies are strengths and which you should focus on first for improvement.

As your coaches, we wish you the best and hope that you will use this workbook and the others to become a better leader. You can also visit our leadership blog at http://blogs.thesidway.com to keep up to date on the progress of our workbooks and learn more about leadership and management topics.

BenchMark Learning International's

4P's Competency Model™

Persuasive Vision

Creativity
Influencing
Inspiration
Motivation
Planning
Strategic Thinking

People Skills

Change Leadership
Commitment to Diversity
Communications
Conflict Management
Interpersonal Skills
Negotiation
Problem Solving
Talent Management
Teamwork

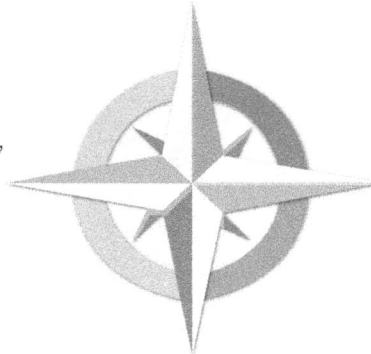

Positive Results

Business Development
Commitment to Quality
Customer Focus
Decision Making
Financial Management
Focus on Results
Technical Skills
Time Management

Personal Character

Courage
Credibility
Followership
Initiative
Integrity
Stress Management
Trust

Appendix F – Using the SID™ Model for Organizational Improvement

After completing this workbook for Time Management, you can see how it helps you individually improve your skills and behaviors. However, we feel that it is important that organizations use this information to change their culture to be more focused on best practices in time management. Individual improvement is a priority, but it is when an organization embraces the effective use of time and work-life balance as their lifeblood that it becomes most impactful in the organization's culture and in the marketplace.

Often, it is the organization itself that drives people to manage their time inefficiently. The organization must support time management principles and encourage all leaders, managers and employees to make the best use of their time. It is certainly in the best interests of the organization to do so.

The following are some ideas to help your organization improve in time management and work-life balance.

- Recommend that all leaders and managers in the organization use this workbook and the SID™ model to improve their individual time management skills and behaviors. If leaders and managers model excellent behaviors, others will follow the lead.

- Evaluate your organization's time management and work-life balance behaviors. You could also develop a survey or conduct interviews to gain information from team members about how well your organization does in this area.

- Reward those individuals who exemplify excellent time management skills and behaviors. This can be done inexpensively with an award, such as a plaque or by giving some other tangible benefit such as a gift certificate. Be sure to communicate this action and the behavior that earned it across the organization.

About Your Coaches

Ben and Sidney McDonald are co-owners of BenchMark Learning International. Both are respected executive coaches and facilitators of leadership programs. Their primary work has been with Fortune 500 corporations and some of the country's leading universities including Dartmouth College, Johns Hopkins Medical University, Illinois Institute of Technology, and Case Western Reserve University.

Corporate clients have included Cisco Systems, CB&I, KBR, Skanska USA, Ericsson, Siemens and others. Both specialize in the design, development and delivery of leadership programs. Both are also experienced leadership development consultants and work with organizations in improving their leadership and talent management systems.

They have held leadership positions in their professional career and have translated this experience into their leadership development programs and executive coaching. Until the founding of BenchMark Learning in 1987, Ben held leadership positions with GTE, McDonnell Douglas, and International Learning Systems. Sidney was a leader at US West for over 17 years prior to joining BenchMark Learning in 1997.

If you have any questions for your coaches on the content of this book, the SID process, or would like ideas to help you or your group exceed expectations in time management, you may contact us at questions@thesidway.com.